# Take Time for the Pain

PILGRIMAGE THROUGH SUFFERING

**HAROLD T. BRYSON**

© 2022

Published in the United States by Nurturing Faith, Macon, GA.

Nurturing Faith is a book imprint of Good Faith Media (goodfaithmedia.org).

Library of Congress Cataloging-in-Publication Data is available.

ISBN: 978-1-63528-181-1

All rights reserved. Printed in the United States of America.

Scripture quotations taken from the (NASB®) New American Standard Bible®, Copyright © 1960, 1971, 1977, 1995, 2020 by The Lockman Foundation. Used by permission. All rights reserved.
www.lockman.org

Cover image by Pradeep Charles on Unsplash.

*To Jane, my wife
With whom it is easier to stay in love
than it was to fall in love*

# Contents

Introduction .................................................................................. 1

Chapter 1: A Personal Pilgrimage .................................................. 9

Chapter 2: Some Helpful Resources ............................................. 21

Chapter 3: Searching for a Cause ................................................. 35

Chapter 4: Noticeable Symptoms .................................................. 49

Chapter 5: Confusing Voices ........................................................ 61

Chapter 6: Searching for Help ...................................................... 75

Chapter 7: Surprising Profits ....................................................... 89

Chapter 8: Ultimate Hope ............................................................ 99

# Introduction

In spring of 1989, a church in Dayton, Ohio, invited me to teach a four-day Bible study. As I traveled to that engagement, I struggled with one of the most painful experiences of my life: three years earlier in June 1986, my wife of twenty-three years moved from our home without my knowledge. Having returned to New Orleans late one night, I entered the house to find that my wife and sons were gone. Most of the furniture was also gone. My wife had left a note on the kitchen counter that read, "I have decided to leave." She left no reason for her departure and no address for where she'd gone. The absence of my family created shock, disbelief, numbness, panic, hopelessness, and many other feelings. I sat in silence throughout the night. I tried to pray. I cried. In my mind, I felt that the tragedy had not happened.

On the third day of my time in Dayton, I experienced an unexpected teachable moment. It happened when I sought diversion from the loneliness of my motel room and spotted the grand opening of a large wholesale store across the street. As I entered the store, the voice of Carly Simon greeted me over the sound system, singing "I Haven't Got Time for the Pain." The lyrics of that song hit me in a strange way. It occurred to me that I hadn't taken my pain honestly—spiritually, theologically, or practically. I thought that the marriage would mend and the pain would go away, and I hoped we would live happily the rest of our days. I substituted fanciful imaginings for hardcore realities. I tried to cover my pain by escaping into my work. I drove my pain deeper into my subconscious, hoping that if I buried it deeply enough, I might forget it was there. But the words of Carly Simon gave me pause. As I evaluated my futile responses to pain, I mentally reversed her lyric with a new realization: "You have to take time for the pain."

My research into pain has opened my eyes to its extensive prevalence. Pain exists everywhere and in everyone, recognizing no gender, ethnicity, or socioeconomic class. It appears in the educated and the uneducated, the beautiful and the plain, the spiritual and the atheistic. It surfaces time and again from infancy to death, unfazed by wealth, success, or power. Human life is frail, and everyone is subject to hurts beyond their power to manage—grief, illness, relational hurt, financial disaster. No human being ever lives without pain.

Learning that one-third of our world's population goes to bed hungry enlarged my view of the prevalence of pain. Watching the news about wars, terrorists, mass murders, and rapists informed me about how tragic life can be. Each day I look at the newspaper and read about people injured or killed in automobile accidents. I also see two to four pages each day of obituary notices listing people who have died. I think often of the pain of the deceased before they died and the pain of relatives after their loved ones have passed.

Massive natural occurrences injure and kill many people. These disasters make headlines, and we reel from the enormous devastation of property and lives. Child abuse represents a crime that leaves physical and emotional hurts. Sexual harassment, exploitation, and assault leave victims to bear not only their trauma but also the burden of a secret. Before my experience in Ohio, I barely blinked over these happenings that brought pain and death. But now, suffering captivates my attention.

Pain and suffering differ in both duration and kind. For some, pain defines most of their lives. It is the first sensation that greets them in the morning and the last that leaves them before they go to sleep. But most people experience scattered bouts of suffering. An illness comes or an accident occurs, and hurt happens. The pain, in most cases, lasts for a specified time before fading away. Different episodes necessitate different lengths of time to heal.

Pain also differs in kind. All kinds of mental, physical, and emotional experiences bring pain, and many wonder what types of incidents bring the most pain. But the reality is that the amount of suffering experienced isn't determined by the type of pain in question. Throughout the course of this book, you will read about my different kinds of pain—an alcoholic father, a broken marriage, and four experiences with cancer. I cannot name the particular event that caused the most pain: each one hurt me deeply.

The more I've watched and listened to the world around me, the more horrible happenings have come to my sight as I've examined the subject of suffering and the experience of pain. Seeing people in hospitals and cancer treatment centers enlightened me to the numerous people suffering physically from diseases, accidents, and sicknesses. Visiting rehabilitation centers focused on helping people with drug and alcohol addictions increased my knowledge about emotional suffering. Going to treatment centers where people with birth defects are housed allowed me to see human beings of all ages suffering from mental challenges. They have to be in a place of care because they cannot care for themselves.

The study of pain and suffering unlocked my ears to the cries for help from people living with all kinds of pain. Seeing the overwhelming presence of pain motivated me to engage in empathetic imagination about the feelings of suffering people. I began to ask, "What are their feelings? What are they saying?" In my imagination as well in my observation and experience, I heard people calling for help. They did not need philosophical facts about suffering. They needed practical help, and they called for assistance to help them cope with or manage their pain.

Sufferers utilize human resources to help manage, reduce, or eliminate their pain. One of the most prominent human efforts involves the attempt to escape pain, and though many escape routes can be tried, two of the most prominent are drugs and alcohol. Prescription drugs for pain can be extremely helpful, but they can also be extremely harmful when abused. Illegal drugs abound, and their primary purpose is to help those who use them escape hurt. Alcohol represents another escape route, offering the illusion of freedom from pain and distress. Both drugs and alcohol help a person get away from the pain for a while, but after a time the chemicals lose their effectiveness, and pain, unshaken, returns.

Sufferers also utilize the human endeavor of mind management to try to manage their pain. Yoga, along with transcendental meditation, involves techniques for controlling the mind and body to avoid distressing or distracting thoughts and promote a peaceful state. In the twentieth century, a New York preacher at the Marble Collegiate Church popularized the art of thinking positive thoughts, and his book *The Power of Positive Thinking* has sold thousands of copies. Physical diversions offer another strategy—physical exercise and work immersion are common, as are recreational activities. The art of managing the mind helps conjure peaceful thoughts for a while, but after time passes, the mind returns to a distressed state.

Over the past three or four decades, sufferers have also organized support groups to cope with stress, strain, and trauma. These groups consist mostly of individuals suffering from the same kind of pain. They meet together and ventilate their feelings. They share findings of what has been beneficial to soothe their suffering. And they practice the art of problem solving and of accepting the things they cannot change.

Ultimately, every human being will come to the place where they realize they are not smart enough or strong enough to cope with the pain. At the end of all human efforts, the cries of the suffering can still be heard: "But where do we get good help?" Fortunately, there is another way. Instead of trusting in what we can do and what other human beings can do, we can open our lives to the divine. From my own testimony and the witness of others, I have found that the best help comes from God.

In the book of Psalms, the psalmist shares about a shepherd's relationship with his sheep. More than likely the writer of the psalm was a shepherd, and he knew the nature of sheep. Shepherding in ancient times didn't consist of putting the sheep in a fenced pasture; rather, the shepherd and the sheep lived together. The shepherd protected the sheep from enemies, provided for their physical needs, and led them to green pastures and still waters. But they still experienced dangers. Wild animals preyed on the sheep. Rugged terrain and steep hills frightened them. Of these experiences, the psalmist wrote, "Even though I walk through the valley of the shadow of death, I fear no evil; for You are with me" (Psalm 23:4a). The great resource and encouragement for believers is the assurance that we do not live alone. We have the promise of God's presence.

Not only is God's presence sensed in times of suffering; God's ability to help is always available. God's power can enable anyone to endure any kind of trouble. God gives strength to cope with pain and suffering. During my darkest times, I received strength and peace that were far beyond me. Paul, the apostle, received strength and peace from God. In the closing years of his life, he was imprisoned in Rome, suffering from hunger and thirst, loneliness and despair. He had many wants, the chief of which was to be released from prison and go preach the gospel. Paul gave a great testimony about God as a source of strength: "my God will supply all your needs according to His riches in glory in Christ Jesus" (Philippians 4:19). God did not give Paul what he wanted, but God did give him what he needed. Sufferers turning to God find that God majors on meeting needs rather than granting human wishes.

My time with pain not only opened my eyes and my ears but also stimulated my mind to ask questions. No emotional feeling produces more inquiries than suffering and pain: Why did God allow my hurt to happen? Why did this happen to me? How can I manage this painful situation? Will God work a miracle to remove my pain? The one question that kept coming to my mind was, "Is there any profit or benefit that I can derive from my pain?"

There seemed to be two potential answers to that last question. One answer could be "no gain to the pain." Lots of people see suffering as an interruption of the freedom to live a happy life. The only results they can see of pain are anxiety, depression, distress, hopelessness, and meaninglessness. The answer of no gain to the pain sees no positive good. Trials and troubles can make you numb to life. They can also make you bitter.

Fortunately, there is another answer to the question about the profit or non-profit of pain. In his book *The Importance of Suffering*, the psychologist James Davies writes about "productive suffering."[1] Davies actually feels that pain can bring gain, improvement, development, progress, growth, and other positive benefits. He claims that suffering and pain can make one wiser and more realistic about life. I add to Davies's word that pain developed more endurance and serenity within me. Of course, suffering does not automatically improve your life; it involves choice and the inner work of learning and growing to help with your adverse circumstances and your negative feelings.

The Bible explains and confirms Professor Davies's idea of productive suffering. The Bible teaches that God uses suffering to put qualitative gains in our lives. My suffering brought me closer to God, but it also tested my connection with God. *Do I have a vital connection with God?* I questioned. I concluded that I did, but I needed to draw closer. The word "relationship" became prominent in my spiritual life. I opened my life more in conversations with God. I acknowledged God's presence in every situation and in every place. I confessed my sins and weaknesses. I even vented my anger, and I am ashamed to say that sometimes that anger was directed toward God.

I allowed God to communicate with me. Of course, I never heard an audible voice, but God did communicate, speaking to me primarily through the Scriptures. At other times God whispered to me in circumstances, through the words of other people, and through inner promptings. God's word became a "lamp to my feet / And a light to my path" (Psalm 119:105). I confess that sometimes my prayers seemed to go nowhere and produce no results. At times my reading of the Bible seemed to be merely routine. But I learned to persevere in praying and reading my Bible, and on occasions God's closeness and communication were evident.

My pain also produced profitable character transformation. During my hardship of hurt, the letter of 1 Peter meant a lot to me. Peter and his readers faced suffering frequently. They lived in an environment not friendly to Christians. Their faith was slandered and maligned. Their social status, family relationships, and even their livelihood were threatened. Peter wrote about the metaphor of a refiner's fire, saying that they suffered "so that the proof of your faith, being more precious than gold which perishes though tested by fire, may be found to result in praise, glory, and honor at the revelation of Jesus Christ" (1 Peter 1:7). Gold is a precious metal, but it can be mixed with impurities. Therefore, it must be refined. When the refiner heats the gold, the heat drives impurities to the surface. These impurities are skimmed off, and the purer gold emerges.

Peter likened the Christians who had saving faith in Jesus Christ to gold filled with impurities. Mixed in with our faith in God are all kinds of impurities unpleasant to God and unbecoming in believers. We have many imperfections. Prejudice, covetousness, unkindness, ungratefulness, criticism, and other flaws exist within us. In most cases we are blind to our blemishes even though they darken our own lives and negatively influence other people.

Then suffering comes along. All of our impurities are revealed, drawn out by trials and suffering just as a refiner's fire draws out the impurities in the gold. Like fire working on gold, suffering can lead us to get rid of some things in our lives and purify and strengthen other things in our lives. Adversity is like a fire. It can make us into a better person. During the early years of my trauma of a relationship break, I collected many negative traits. But when I took time for my pain in a serious and spiritual manner, I became a better person. Even my closer friends told me that many bad qualities were eliminated from my life and many good qualities were added.

Pain became profitable to me in that hardships reminded me of the true values in life. Suffering has a way of transforming our relationship with good things into a relationship with more important things. Making money, gaining power, striving for position and prestige, developing a career, engaging in recreation, and other pursuits can become too important to us. I know that preaching, teaching, and writing took too much of my time, and I gave priority to these activities. But when I was devastated by a relational break, I began to change my priorities, and I came to see that trouble taught me the lesson of true values. Trouble can be an opportunity to invest more of our hope and meaning in God, family, and other people. These new investments fortify us for future hardships. New values can appear in our lives and bring greater joy.

Pain and suffering became profitable to me in that hurt opened me to sympathy and compassion toward others. I became open to others who shared my type of pain, learning that sufferers could be what Henri Nouwen called "wounded healers." Nouwen writes in his book *The Wounded Healer* that those who have been hurt can help others who have been hurt.[2] Paul wrote about the God of comfort, "who comforts us in all our affliction so that we will be able to comfort those who are in any affliction with the comfort with which we ourselves are comforted by God" (2 Corinthians 1:4). Indeed, through my own suffering, I learned that sufferers can become comforters to others.

Suffering drives us to God, who offers unfathomable comforts and gives us a deeper view of who God is. God gives us new experiences of love, self-knowledge, and growth. God gives us insight into life. What does God do to comfort us? God wants us to share our comfort with others and together grow through troubles into the people God wants us to become.

This book grew out of a teachable moment in Dayton, Ohio. The experience motivated me to deeply probe my experience with pain and to study the subject of pain academically. A journey began with acknowledging, confessing, reading, studying, listening, observing, and reflecting to learn more about my own experience with pain and the subject of pain as a whole. The book has been completed, but the journey continues. There is still much left to learn.

This book has a different style than any other book I have written. It contains autobiography, confessions, introspections, and other personal matters. Throughout, I am transparent in my feelings and candid about how other people have influenced my pain. Accompanying this candor is my diligent attempt to refrain from blaming others and making myself the innocent one.

The opening chapter of this book relates my personal journey with pain, while chapter 2 discusses helpful resources for understanding and dealing with pain. My educational pursuit of the subject yielded chapters on symptoms of pain (ch. 3), the cause of pain (ch. 4), and some confusing assessments of our pain from other people (ch. 5). Chapter 6 examines seeking and receiving help in coping with pain, and chapter 7 outlines our duty as sufferers to help others in pain. The book closes with a chapter on hope: believers look forward to a future with no more pain.

No book is a solo production, and this one is not an exception. I cannot name all of the people who have encouraged me "not to waste my sorrows." They wanted me to write a book about my experiences and insights with pain. Many friends listened to me and assisted me in writing this book. A wise professional counselor helped me to assess my pain and grow from it. Some people I did not regard as friends chose to offer sympathy and empathy for my hurts. They listened to my distresses without assessments or judgments. Colleagues at Mississippi College and Carson-Newman University acted as "priests" in my pain and educators in my writing. Surprisingly, many of my students stood alongside me when I hurt, and they helped me enormously. Thanks to Lynda Street, a co-worker with me at Mississippi College, for encouraging me to write the book. Gratitude also goes to Katie Little for her proof-reading and helpful suggestions. Thanks to all who shared with me their walk through divorce and illnesses.

No one deserves more recognition than my wife. We married on May 21, 2005, and began a journey of close companionship. She has amazing spiritual and practical insights. In the writing of this book, Jane listened, evaluated, disagreed, encouraged, affirmed, tolerated, and motivated me. I thank God for our marriage. We are learning together about life's journey, and it is quite fun. Many of my close friends say to me, "Jane is the best thing to happen to you." I agree.

When I thought I wanted to write a book on pain, I began to think of a purpose for publishing such a book. Numerous verbs came to mind: share, inform, interpret, educate, challenge, think. The one verb that took preeminence over all others was "help." I found help from God and from many people, and I wanted to write a book to help people take time for the pain.

The very best part is that we aren't in it alone.

### Notes

[1] James Davies, T*he Importance of Suffering: The Value and Meaning of Emotional Discontent* (New York: Routledge, 2012), 188.

[2] Henry Nouwen, *The Wounded Healer: Ministry in Contemporary Society* (New York: Doubleday and Company, Inc., 1972).

# Chapter 1

# A Personal Pilgrimage

Life is a journey. It may be compared to taking a trip in a car. Of course, before the journey can begin, the traveler must decide where to go. Then the traveler must choose the roads to travel. I personally prefer to travel on interstate highways the whole trip. I want the roads to be smooth and sparsely traveled. As the journey continues, I want to see beautiful sights with green meadows, flowing rivers and streams, and majestic hills or mountains. In the spring and summer, I want to see green grass. In the fall, I want to see a kaleidoscope of colors with the changing of the leaves.

When we travel by car, we do not want to be interrupted by road construction or traffic congestion. However, road travel cannot be filled only with idyllic situations. Sometimes we make wrong turns, and they divert us from where we need to go. Careless driving from other drivers keeps us alert to their recklessness. Accidents along the way hinder our travel time. And even the best cars have flat tires and engine trouble.

Traveling by automobile offers an appropriate image for the living of our days on the journey of life. We want life to be smooth and trouble free, but no matter what precautions we take, problems are sure to arise. We can work to be healthy, but illnesses still come; we can work to be safe, but attack and assault still find a way in. No amount of striving and planning can prevent grief over the deaths of relatives and friends, relational betrayals, financial disasters, moral failures, or other hardships. Natural disasters erupt, accidents happen, and property loss occurs. Traveling through life does not mean we shall be greeted solely with life's joys and pleasures; we will also encounter life's suffering and pain. No one travels through life immune to trouble and hurt.

My journey through life has lasted more than seven decades. I have loved my family, enjoyed my career, and experienced good health for most of this time. I have experienced pleasures too numerous to mention, and for the most part life has been good. But a severe bump hit me in 1986 when I suffered a relational break with my wife. This event caused me the greatest shock and the deepest pain in my life to that point. It brought more questions, hurt, and self-examinations than any other event I had faced. Bothersome emotional feelings plagued me: anxiety, despair, fear, rejection, hopelessness, guilt, and many other negative feelings. Later in the story I will say more about this traumatic event.

As I related earlier, in my deep pain I made a decision influenced by Carly Simon's song "I Haven't Got Time for the Pain." Her song may be the wish of every person, but every person must take time for the pain. After my decision to study and think about my pain, ideas and feelings flooded my mind. I wanted to investigate more. But where would I start? Early in the process, it dawned on me that I should review my life's journey and identify the different types of pain I had experienced. I gave serious attention to the relational break, but the more I looked at my life, the more I realized that suffering and pain had always been a part of it.

My study of developmental psychology helped me organize my life journey. The study divides life into stages or eras. The same basic person exists in each stage, but as life progresses, the passage from one state to another reflects diversities in individuals. I choose to tell my pilgrimage with pain in five stages: infancy and childhood, adolescence, young adulthood, middle adulthood, and senior adulthood. Of course, I do not intend to narrate my entire life story; hurt has not consumed my entire life, and no one era was filled completely with pain. Rather, I have selected significant incidents within the five stages to tell about my experiences with pain.

The first stage of my life was infancy and childhood. This era began with my birth and lasted until I was thirteen. Of course, each of us begins the saga of life in exactly the same way—through the trauma of being separated from the warmth and security of a mother's womb to exist on our own. No one remembers the trauma of birth. I certainly do not. In fact, I do not remember many experiences during my infancy and recall only a few from my early childhood. During my childhood, I became conscious of some of life's happenings—the pleasant and the horrible, the enjoyable and the disagreeable, the happy times and the hurting times. But only a few of these conscious happenings remain in my mind.

So how do we know about the events that occur during our infancy and childhood? I learned about that era mostly from stories my parents told me about my growing up. They related incidents where I had pain. They told me that when I was an infant, I had a problem with colic. They also told me of illnesses I had such as measles, whooping cough, chicken pox, and influenza. I barely remember some of the pain from these illnesses. I do remember that I did not like pain from the earliest times of life, and I wanted the hurt to go away.

The events of my life from thirteen to eighteen are more memorable. During that time, I developed physically, intellectually, emotionally, and socially—transitions that brought growing pains. My adolescence required many adjustments for my parents, too: they had the delicate task of letting up on a relationship without letting it go completely. It also meant that I had to pick up responsibility and walk forward in my life without completely letting go of my parents.

During my teenage years, some religious ideas brought me extreme emotional pain. Ideas about God being angry and wrathful caused me to be afraid. I also heard a lot about the "signs of the time." People predicted the end of the world by interpreting current events, and these people spoke of the end in the tone of God's vengeance and wrath. These reports about the end caused me to dread the time to come, fueling my anxiety rather than my comfort. Lots of legalistic thinking existed during my adolescent years as well. Church leaders and others told me what I should and should not do. It was religion by the rules, and acceptance was unattainable. Feeling this lack of doing or not doing brought uneasiness and doubt to my mind.

These religious ideas contributed to my unhealthy emotions. Being afraid of God brought bad feelings about a good God. Extreme emphasis on the so-called "last days" distorted a comforting time for believers and encouraged negative feelings about the future. Fortunately, relief from these bothersome ideas came in my later teen years. My therapy involved diligent Bible reading and intensive Bible study. I began to see a more realistic and enjoyable picture of God—one of a loving Father. Additional involvement with Scripture helped me see that God will bring history to a close. Believers will experience beyond this life a perfect expression of the life they have in Christ now. They will live in a perfect environment without any suffering or evil. My study of the Scripture taught me that God's acceptance comes by grace rather than by obeying rules. Over the years I have been helped with my fears and anxiety about God's nature, the end of the world, and a rule-based religion.

During my stage of adolescence, a struggle within my immediate family brought me great pain. While some people knew about our situation, what I now share with you was mostly kept a secret until the latter part of my middle years. I reluctantly disclose to my readers the secret of my dad's involvement with alcohol. I never knew him to be a social drinker in my childhood or adolescent years. Evidently, the habit developed secretly and then became more regular.

For some reason or reasons known only to my dad, he engaged in intermittent bouts with excessive alcoholic consumption. These episodes occurred three to four times a year. Each excessive situation gradually turned my dad into a different person. In his normal, sober life he was kind, considerate, generous, respecting, and loving to my mother and me. But under the influence of alcohol, he became a man filled with rage and criticism. I was puzzled over these two paradoxical behaviors. Surprisingly, Dad directed some of his rage during alcoholic bouts toward Mom and me. I could not understand what was happening. This was the father I dearly loved, and he told me in sober times that he loved me. He took me fishing frequently. I traveled with him on his business routes. On these journeys he told me stories from his childhood and from his service in the Navy. He also taught me how to work in his automobile parts store and how to treat customers.

But Dad's alcoholic bouts came without any warning. Mom and I learned to predict when "a night of terror" was coming. During those times of excessive drinking, Dad was usually late coming home from work. His tardiness indicated that we had a tough night coming. Mom and I spent many nights watching and waiting for his truck to appear in the driveway. This time of waiting caused me to be anxious and to dread his arrival.

Soon after my father entered the house, he initiated a frightening rage. He spoke angry and hurtful words to my mother, who took his abusive words with silence. She never tried to defend herself. Her only relief was a fixed stare on the floor and the shedding of many tears. Dad also spoke those unkind words to me. In the first of his alcoholic bouts, I verbally defended my mother and myself, but I quickly gave up on that. I, too, found relief in silence. My silence concealed my anxiety and fear. At times I worried about my dad turning to physical violence, though thankfully he never did. Still, his words lodged in my mind. They descended into my subconscious. For years, the memory of my dad's words and actions replayed constantly in my mind.

I remember the long nights of terror. I couldn't sleep, replaying Dad's words as I lay in bed. The next morning my eyes were red and swollen from the flow of tears and the lack of sleep. At school, teachers and friends noticed that something was wrong with me, but I dared not disclose the secret. Instead, I said, "I have a cold." Mom and I both practiced the conspiracy of silence and shared our pain together.

The morning after each "night of terror," my dad returned to his sober self. Each morning afterwards, he expressed regret for his behavior. He cried and begged Mom and me to forgive him. Each time he promised that he would never do it again, but the nights of terror continued. My mother and I forgave him after each episode, and we hoped that his promise would come true. Mom continued to love him and to forgive him. From her I saw the example of unwarranted love and unlimited forgiveness.

A transition eventually came in Dad's life. A friend invited him to attend an Alcoholics Anonymous (AA) meeting with him. Dad consented to go, and he continued to attend. Mom and I began to notice a difference. The time between alcoholic episodes grew longer. My dad got excited about AA. The people with whom he met shared his struggle. They were hurting and needed help. They openly confessed their problem to each other. The attendees listened with understanding and compassion, refusing to judge each other. The fun-loving father I once knew became present again. He remained sober for ten years after his first AA meeting. No nights of terror happened from that day until his death ten years later. Dad and I returned to fishing trips. We attended football and basketball games together with Mom. He enjoyed his grandchildren. Thank God that people can change! Thank God for people in Alcoholics Anonymous!

The nights of terror did stop, but my memories of those nights continued to replay in my mind. Anxiety and fear lingered within me, and in my college years, I decided to go to a counselor about my family situation. In counseling, I unloaded the burden of my secret. This counselor first asked me to make a genogram of my immediate family system. She wanted the names of my family members, but she also wanted me to characterize their personalities and their life behaviors. The counselor taught me some valuable truths about family systems. She gave me two theories: One theory advocates that behavior in the immediate family system determines the children's behavior. The second theory proposes that family systems do not determine children's behavior but that the behavior in the system influences them. She assured me that my father's actions did not determine the way I lived, but she related how I could be influenced by his behavior.

The counselor gave me two assignments for future sessions. First, she wanted me to read Claudia Black's book *Children of Alcoholics*. This book helped me see how other people hurt the same way I did. Throughout her book, Black offers practical help in dealing with damaged emotions.[1] The second assignment the counselor gave me was to read David Seamands's book *Healing of Memories*. In this book I learned that memories, good or bad, are a part of our lives.[2] Seamands led me to practice selective memories. Of course, I could not help remembering many of the bad memories from Dad's alcoholic episodes. But I selectively chose to remember the good memories with Dad. Now I am years away from that time in my life, and I rarely think of the bad times. I choose to recall the good times.

The years of my dad's alcoholic incidents were bad times in my life. I am glad he got help and decided to live a different life. My counselor and friends helped me to heal from the damaged emotions of fear, anxiety, and distress. The Lord helped me get through the dark times. It was painful in the moment, but the pain has been healed.

When I passed from adolescence to young adulthood, I thought my pain would lessen. But I soon learned that there is no graduation exercise for pain. It continues in our lives in various lengths and depths for the rest of our journey. Young adulthood brought challenges for different life changes, and transitions characterized my early years as an adult. I left home to go to college. Being away from home brought both the joy of freedom and the agony of homesickness. College challenged me to think and to study more. While I was in college, I chose the career of Christian ministry. That decision led me to attend seminary after college, and those graduate studies in turn brought greater academic challenges.

After graduating from seminary, I met and married the person who would become my wife for twenty-three years. Married life meant adjustment to caring and providing for another person. Three years after marriage, we had a son, and thirteen months later, we had another son. Married life did not bring traumatic pain during the first two decades, but pain came twenty-three years later in my middle years.

The early adult years certainly did not ensure an idyllic, tranquil era. Adjustments, anxieties, and annoyances came during this era along with joys and delights. These adult years did not bring long-lasting and deeply hurtful pain, but they did involve experiences that required learning and adapting. Learning to be married requires adjustments. Preparing educationally for a career and learning to practice that career brings vocational challenges as well as the need for financial provisions. Being a parent brought joy, but it also brought responsibilities. Balancing the changes during my young adulthood did create anxiety, fear, and sometimes distress. But I do not remember any traumatic happenings causing deep and lasting hurt.

After the young adult years, I passed into the middle years. I would say that from thirty-five to forty-five represented one of the most enjoyable times of my life. I found fulfillment in my career. I thoroughly loved teaching in the seminary and preaching in many different churches. I enjoyed watching our sons play three high school sports. My wife and I saw them play almost every game. During this time I often said, "Life doesn't get any better than this."

But a decade into my middle years, I faced emotional upheavals. Psychologists label the time of forty-five to sixty-five years of age as one of the most challenging stages of life. My first hurtful experience of this time was the sudden death of my father. I grieved deeply over his passing, and as I continued to grieve one year later, the most traumatic event of my life occurred: unexpected separation from my wife of twenty-three years. The event happened when I returned from a four-day Bible study in Houston, Texas. On a late Wednesday night—June 4, 1986—I drove home from the airport, and when I walked into our house, my wife, sons, and furniture were gone. I faced an empty house. There was a note on the kitchen counter: "I have decided to leave." My wife stated no prior warning or reason. She left no address of where she and our sons had gone. I sat on the floor of our house in a state of shock, numbness, and disbelief, feeling paralyzed. Tears flowed for most of that night and for days and years to come. It seemed as if that night had not happened. It also seemed that it would never end.

Several days after that distressing night, people began to contact me. Many of my students came to see me and to pray with me. Several married students invited me to their apartments for meals. Some of the people I thought to be my friends avoided me. Others I barely knew reached out to me in compassion and concern. The seminary where I taught assured me that I could stay on two conditions: I could not date, and I could not remarry. Those conditions deeply hurt me because my primary concern was to work to restore my relationship with my wife. Actually, I became angry over these stipulations. My wife had been gone for less than a week, and it bothered me that some would think that dating and remarrying were on my mind.

Two weeks after the separation, I called my wife. I told her that I loved her and that I wanted to help mend whatever problem she had with me. I asked her how I could help, but her only reply to my question was, "We just drifted away." She stayed separated from me for several years—a time of tension, distress, loneliness, anxiety, and confusion. Three years and six months after she left, a law official delivered divorce papers to me. Attempts at reconciliation failed. Being rejected brought me great pain. I thought we could mend our marriage, but she thought differently.

After my wife left, I soon began to experience life-style changes. Two weeks after my wife's departure, my sons contacted me and wanted to live with me. They came back, and I began the challenging life of being a single parent. Planning and preparing meals for me and for two young men with bottomless pits presented the greatest challenge. Life handed me another vocation along with my teaching and preaching. My daily routine took on domestic duties such as washing clothes, dusting furniture, cleaning floors, and other tasks. One of my sons departed for college and the other son stayed home and attended college. A bright spot for my singleness came when my college son came home and joined us again. We spent week-ends in the spring and days in the summer fishing and water skiing. It was precious togetherness. Actually during this time of singleness my sons and I became closer. We talked more, laughed a lot, and cried occasionally. When my sons were not with me, I experienced the exaggerated anguish of aloneness. I could not get interested in television shows or sporting events. I became restless at night. I had a hard time getting to sleep and staying asleep. Many nights I sat stoically in my chair for hours unable to relax or focus. I could only think of the pain. Life changed, but I managed with God's help, the companionship of my sons, and my encouraging friends to survive singleness.

Several years passed and our marital status remained the same. My wife continued to communicate to me that she did not know what she wanted to do. I felt that I was in a state of limbo with great frustration. I lived each day hoping that reconciliation would happen but also dreading the possibility of being served with divorce papers. My emotional state worsened as I fell deeper into distress, depression, and loneliness. I lived each moment with the horrible pain of being rejected by the person I had married. Mentally, I reasoned constantly about what my wife was going to do and how the situation might affect my ministerial career. I continued to teach and preach but with a two-track mind: on one track I concentrated on the explanation and application of scripture, but on the other track I hurt deeply in my innermost being. The pain would not go away.

Three days into my teaching engagement in Dayton, I experienced an unexpected teachable moment. The moment happened when I sought diversion from the loneliness of my motel room. I walked outside the motel and spotted the announcement of a grand opening of a large wholesale store. I crossed the street to go to the opening, and as I entered the door, I heard Carly Simon singing, "I haven't got time for the pain." The lyrics of that popular song caught my attention in a strange way. I began to admit that I had not taken time for my pain honestly, spiritually, theologically, or practically. All along my painful journey, I felt that our marriage would mend and the pain would go away. I hoped that we would live happily together for the rest of our days. During the years of separation, I substituted fanciful imaginings for hardcore realities. I tried to cover my hurt by escaping into my work. I drove my pain deeper into the subconscious, hoping that if I buried it deep enough, I might forget my hurts. But the words of Carly Simon gave me another perspective. As I evaluated my futile responses to pain, I reversed her words with a new realization: "You have to take time for the pain."

Crowded into the years of marital separation, another hurtful situation entered my life: my mother was diagnosed with Alzheimer's disease just a few months after my father died. I began to see this wonderful woman deteriorate in mind and in body, and seeing her condition worsen was incredibly painful. Several years after her diagnosis, she did not know me. Because I was an only child, I had the responsibility of ensuring she was cared for. I remember late one night I cried out to God. "Lord, I have had enough with the departure of my wife, the death of my father, and the illness of my mother." I can truthfully say that the Lord gave me strength to endure during those painful times.

What immediate lessons did I learn from that teachable moment? I reviewed my failed attempts to help with pain. I could no longer escape the hurt by trying to engage in other thoughts. I could no longer neglect the pain hoping that I would soon forget it and it would go away. I could no longer substitute my work or my recreational pursuits for the pain. I faced the reality of deep hurt, and I made a monumental decision to exercise serious disciplines to take time for the pain. These self-enforced practices involved engaging in thoughtful Bible study, academic research, personal introspection, and insights that others grappling with pain shared with me.

The moment in Dayton was not just a casual experience. It was a life-changing time that began in the spring of 1989. I embarked on the pilgrimage of processing my pain and learning as much as I could about myself and the experience of pain. It led to a greater awareness of God in my life, and I began to sense God more. I confessed faults and feelings. I searched my life to see where I had failed in my marriage. I acknowledged my helplessness and called out for God's help. My closer connection with God helped me with the martial separation as well was with other subsequent hurts. I would not have imagined that the time in Dayton would have such enduring and therapeutic effects. That flash of influence continues to follow me to the present day.

I lived through the tribulation of divorce and reached the time known as the senior years. Like any other era of my life, the senior years have brought both agonies and ecstasies. Overwhelming feelings of happiness and fulfillment marked the beginning of this era with my marriage to Jane on May 21, 2005. Our years together have been both fulfilling and fun. Of course, during our marriage Jane and I have faced both joys and sorrows together with God's help. Our marriage created a blended family with four children and seven grandchildren. We have enjoyed each person of the blending.

Retirement has also arrived during my senior years, helping me to slow down, diversify my activities, and reflect. In these years, I have thought more about being rather than about having or achieving. It has been gratifying to know that my worth comes ultimately from God's love and care for me. I have thought about the times when God has been actively at work in my life for good. This work involved the producing of God's character in my life. And it isn't only the pleasures and the successes that bear the mark of God's hands, but all events—the bad as well as the good. With maturity I have been able to accept the bittersweet quality of my hurtful experiences rather than resent them. An old Arab proverb states, "All sunshine makes a desert." I have found that to be true.

Along with the ecstasies of the senior years, there have been agonies. I have noticed the misery of diminished physical powers. I have been saddened with the increasing number of deaths of my contemporaries. I have sensed the agony of separation from my former teaching colleagues. Agonizing health problems have also hit me hard in my senior years. Just before I entered this era, I was diagnosed with prostate cancer. The "C" word frightened me. The diagnosis made me face my mortality more than any other event in my life. Thankfully, a competent surgeon removed my cancer, and I needed no chemo or radiation treatments. More than fifteen years have passed since my surgery, and while I have been tested each year, the cancer has not appeared again in that area of my body.

But cancer would not lie down and be quiet. Fifteen years after my prostate cancer, I was diagnosed with thyroid cancer. Again, another competent surgeon removed the diseased organ, and a skilled endocrinologist gave me a radioactive iodine treatment. The process worked. A body scan concluded that I had no more cancer in that area of my body.

Several months passed as I enjoyed the freedom won from a fight with cancer. A common sore throat motivated me to see a doctor. He treated me for ten days with antibiotics, but the soreness did not go away. So the doctor ordered a lymph node aspiration, which led to a diagnosis of throat cancer. This diagnosis led to surgery for diseased lymph nodes, which in turn led to four chemotherapy treatments and thirty-five radiation treatments. This was a time of trauma. I experienced debilitating nausea. Because I could not swallow, a feeding tube was inserted into my stomach. My wife fed me through this tube for several months. The nausea, the fatigue, and the continuous treatments brought me great distress. I struggled with negative feelings of depression and even death. I felt isolated from the outside, healthy world.

After six months of procedures, I began to recover. Life became enjoyable again. I could eat. I could attend worship, go to ball games, and go fishing. But during a six-month check of my throat, a PET scan disclosed something suspicious on my left lung. A biopsy concluded that I had lung cancer. When the radiation oncologist gave me the diagnosis, I became disappointed over a second cancer diagnosis in six months' time. Immediately after giving me the diagnosis, my oncologist said, "I have good news. We can get it." Those words gave me optimism for life. For five months, I had four chemo treatments and thirty-five radiation treatments. As I write these words, a CT scan has disclosed that the treatments were successful.

The cancers created great agony in my life. The diagnoses and treatments rank high on the physical and emotional scales of pain. The cancers equal or excel my hurt when my marriage failed, and each discovery of cancer created excessive fear and anxiety within me. The chemo, the radiation, and the surgeries caused me great pain. The chemo combined with the radiation caused numerous episodes of nausea and fatigue.

Dread became a prominent sensation as I faced procedures. I cringed over forthcoming biopsy reports. I struggled with the uneasiness of the unknown. I anguished over every blood test and its results. Strange feelings of isolation and loneliness came to me when I saw myself separated from a healthy world. I confess that, periodically, I thought about the possibility of my death. I had a sense of helplessness greater than I had ever experienced—my life was in the hands of radiologists, oncologists, and other doctors. I could do nothing but depend on their skills. My greatest help during the months of cancer procedures was the Lord. I claimed Psalm 121:1b–2a: "From whence shall my help come? My help comes from the LORD, Who made heaven and earth."

Death will come to me in my senior years. There is no other stage of earthly life after this. Knowing that my death will inevitably come, I hold some truths to help me with my passing. God has provided for my needs during my earthly existence, and I know that God will provide for my needs when I exit this earthly life. Death is an exit, but it is also an entrance: I will pass through the door of death and enter a new and better life—a perfect life with God and with God's people. Immediately after I pass through the door of death, my pain will cease, and I shall experience pain "no more."

### Notes

[1] Claudia Black, *Children of Alcoholics: As Youngsters, Adolescents, Adults* (New York: Ballantine Books, 1981).

[2] David Seamands, *Healing of Memories* (Aurora, IL: Scripture Press Publications, 1985).

# Chapter 2

# Some Helpful Resources

Every journey in life requires resources. If you plan to go hiking in the mountains, you need the right shoes and gear. If you take a trip to the beach, you need a swimsuit, sunscreen, and other items. If you plan to take a ski trip, you need warm clothing and ski equipment.

There are other types of journeys. Some go on educational pilgrimages—they may enroll in a degree program or study a subject on their own. Such an endeavor may include the use of a computer, books, or other academic resources. Other people go on spiritual pilgrimages. They long to know God better and to connect more intimately with God. They long to get in touch with their inner being. Those who go seeking intimacy with God and insight into their inner being might take the Bible, some religious writings, and a blank notebook to use for journaling.

On a Tuesday in October 1989, I began a journey to learn about pain. A devastating relational break caused horrendous hurt both physically and emotionally. Something had to happen for me to function and to grow. The Carly Simon song "I Haven't Got Time for the Pain" stirred a thought within me not to ignore my pain but to explore it. Hearing her song caused me to think that I *did* have to take time for the pain. I immediately embarked on a journey to examine my encounter with pain, searching for resources beyond my emotions and life experiences. My pursuit began and continued with reflecting, confessing, owning, and analyzing my feelings, and I resolved to make the pursuit personal, academic, psychological, philosophical, and spiritual. I wanted to go further with the subject of pain than my personal feelings of hurt.

Throughout my journey, I used four primary resources to gain insight as well as therapy. The first resource I used was the Bible. It became my most informative source to learn about pain. One of my former Old Testament professors suggested that I read carefully all of the psalms to learn about pain and suffering, and as I did, many of my life experiences came to light. In his book titled *God in Man's Experience*, A. Leonard Griffith also helped me to observe life's experiences through the lens of the psalms. Griffith wrote that the psalmists were people who consciously brought God into their experiences, and in so doing, they found that God did for them what no one else could do. Griffith wrote about how the psalms have remained popular and influential through the centuries, touching basic human experiences and relating them to God's involvement in life.[1]

Herman Gunkel, a specialist in the book of Psalms, arranged the 150 psalms according to types. He saw definable types of psalms with fairly consistent form and content, assuming that psalms of the same type came from similar life settings in ancient Israel. Gunkel grouped the psalms into five major types: hymns, community laments, individual laments, individual psalms of thanksgiving, and royal psalms. The second largest psalm type according to Gunkel consisted of lamentation amid stress and difficulty. Of the 150 psalms, 56 involved both individual and corporate lament.[2]

Reading and studying the lament psalms afforded me insight into my own pain and into the pain of others. I identified with the feelings of the psalmists along with their faith and hope. The psalms reflect the idea of the presence of God in times of difficulty. In these hardships, one can learn of God speaking, whispering, shouting, or remaining silent—but always present. The psalmists reflected a human honesty with God. They made intense pleas, asked profound questions, made honest confessions, verbalized straightforward complaints, expressed the presence of doubt, and cried for help. The psalms help us to see ourselves and to see God as God is. The psalms, especially the lament psalms, help us to learn about the thoughts and actions of hurting people.

The book of Job is another excellent biblical resource for learning about pain and suffering. Many Old Testament scholars date the book of Job as the oldest book in the Bible. With that thought, one might think that such an old book cannot be relevant to the twenty-first century. Reading the book of Job, however, brought amazement and insight to me about how the subject of innocent suffering spoken to people centuries ago still speaks to current readers. In his book *Where Is God When It Hurts?* Philip Yancey wrote, "The questions of Job voiced eloquently have not faded away. They have grown even louder and shriller over the centuries."[3] The book of Job raised many questions for me to ponder: Why do good people suffer?

Why is evil allowed in the world? What kind of God rules the world? I found in the story of Job emotional and dramatic realness communicated with intellectual, philosophical, and practical expertise.

The writer of the book of Job opens with an introduction of the man Job. The narrator begins by letting readers know that Job was an incredibly good and godly man. He was a good husband and a caring father of seven sons and three daughters. No one could make a charge against Job in any area of his life. He was materially successful and physically healthy. Behind the story, the narrator lets readers know something that Job did not know. Readers learn that Satan, the accuser, alleges that Job is in a relationship with God merely for the benefits. In other words, Satan insinuates that Job is serving God for what he can get from God. The accuser challenges the Lord to take away Job's benefits, claiming that he will then cease to serve God.

As the story progresses, God allows Satan to test Job. God gives Satan permission to allow pain and suffering into Job's life. In the story line there is no hint of a dualistic view of the world, in which there are two equal and opposite forces of good and evil. The narrator of the book tells the story with God completely in charge—Satan can only go so far. Not only does the narrator present God as being in complete control; he makes it clear that God is not the one inflicting the tragedies on Job. Disasters one after the other affect Job's life: he loses his wealth and all of his children; he loses his health. God does not enjoy seeing Job experiencing such hurt. Job's life of goodness makes these afflictions hard to understand and to take. The disasters seem senseless and unfair.

In the story, Job has three friends from the East. Their names are Eliphaz, Bildad, and Zophar. Upon hearing the news of Job's misfortunes, these friends journey to visit and comfort him. When they arrive and see Job, they do not know him. His condition and appearance have been altered by his calamities. When they recognize him, they are overcome with grief. They express their sorrow over Job by weeping aloud, rending their robes, and sprinkling dust on their heads. Then for a symbolic seven days and nights they sit on the ground by Job in silence, a picture of abject grief.

At last, Job breaks the silence. He curses the day of his birth and expresses the wish that he had never been born. After Job's speech, his friends talk with him. They make several speeches, many of which Job answers. Numerous allusions to God in nature and deep insights into the meaning of human experience characterize the dialogue. Throughout the conversations, the problem with Job's friends is their reasoning for why Job, an apparently innocent and righteous person, should have experienced such unparalleled suffering and loss. All three friends advance the same argument, which was the orthodox explanation of suffering in those days. Suffering, according to these friends, was God's punishment for sin. If a person did well, peace and prosperity would follow. But if a person did evil, suffering would occur. Job's friends recommend that he admit and confess his sins. They felt that his extreme suffering indicated his great sin.

Throughout the conversations between Job and his friends, he affirms his innocence. Though he admits that he is not perfect before God, he insists that his punishment is far more than his sins and failures deserve. Like many people in pain, Job questions, "What have I done, that this trouble should happen to me?" The dialogue between Job and his friends continues this theme. Time and time again Job cries, "If only God were here, he would vindicate me and tell me why these misfortunes have come to me." Likewise, his friends say more than once, "If only God were here, he would side with us and show up Job as a great sinner." Both sides seem to want God to settle the argument and answer the basic question, "Why do people suffer?" Everyone wants an answer to that question—"Why?"

The conversation between Job and his friends lasts for a long time. In fact, in the book of Job, the dialogue dominates the bulk of the material (chapters 3 through 37). After the interruption of a philosopher named Elihu, the argument seems to be finished. It has seemingly been a dialogue in despair; all that human wisdom could say on the subject of suffering has been said. Then a dramatic turn comes in the Job narrative: across the stage of the drama comes a whirlwind, and out of the whirlwind God speaks. God takes center stage in the drama and discusses God's ways with human beings. The words of God continue from chapter 38 to chapter 41.

God begins speaking by becoming the interrogator. Job has been questioning God, and now it becomes God's time to ask Job questions. "Then the LORD answered Job from the whirlwind and said, …Now tighten the belt on your waist like a man, And I shall ask you, and you inform me!" (Job 38:1, 3). As we read the first speech of God from the whirlwind, we find something unexpected. God says none of the things we expect. God does not speak a word about the problem that has been under discussion for the past thirty-six chapters or mention the meaning of suffering. At first, the speech of God seems irrelevant.

God asks: Where were you when I laid the foundation of the world? Who decided how big the world should be? Who determined where the sea should stop and the land begin? Do you cause the day to end and the night to come? Can you make thunder, lightning, or the wind to blow in any direction? Do you understand how the animals regulate their lives?

Such are the questions God asks Job, about forty in number. The questions reflect a survey of nature to show the glory of God. Most of the questions in Job 38 deal with inanimate nature—the creation of the world, the sea and the land, the changes of weather, and the sun and stars. Meanwhile, most of the questions in Job 39 are about animals—the mountain goat, the wild ass, the ostrich, the horse, the hawk, and the eagle. The purpose behind the questions is not to answer the problem under discussion but to give Job and his friends a vision of the glory of God.

God speaks not only to Job but also to his friends, disclosing the fact that it is impossible to understand all the mysteries of the universe. The philosophers had reduced God's ways to neat syllogisms, and Job fretted because he could not reduce God's ways to his finite frame of mind. God gave both Job and his friends a glimpse of God's greatness, mystery, and glory. Instead of learning the abstract truth they thought they needed, they received the presence of God as the answer to their needs.

We desperately need this vision of God in the midst of the evil of our world. We need to look up, as John the apostle did on the isle of Patmos, and see that the Lord God omnipotent reigns above the cruel powers of Rome. We need to see every pain that penetrates our lives in the light of the all-powerful and all-loving God. Just because we are confused about our situation does not mean we should think that God has lost control of the world.

God's speech influenced Job. His pride and self-righteousness were overshadowed by the vision of God. He stopped questioning, and in the presence of God he learned trust and humility. His questions about his reasons for suffering and justice remained unanswered, but a new dimension entered his consciousness: that of God's eternal wisdom and power. He began to take his mind off himself and put it on the great Creator.

In chapter 40, God speaks a second time (40:6–41:34). Job has fallen silent before God, but he has not revealed a readiness to submit his stubborn will to God's control. In the second speech God communicates to Job about his real sin: "Will you really nullify My judgment? Will you condemn Me so that you may be justified?" (Job 40:8). In insisting on his own righteousness, Job has indicted the justice and goodness of God. Job's sin was setting himself up as the judge of God, and with stinging irony, God rebukes his self-righteousness. "If you are as great as you think you are," God says, "then you put on all the splendor of deity; you take over the task of bringing righteousness and justice in the world, since you seem to think you can do it so much better than I! You be God, if you think you know how to run the universe, and I will bow down and worship you!" God wanted Job to realize that he was not the Creator but the created.

God resumes questioning in a second speech. In this part of the speech recorded in chapter 41, we find long descriptions of two creatures called Behemoth and Leviathan. Behemoth is translated "hippopotamus" and Leviathan "crocodile." These are not ordinary animals; thus, they seem to be two symbolic creatures that played a significant role in ancient mythology. These creatures appear to be mythological representatives of the great forces of disunity and chaos that God brought under control. They communicate one majestic thought: the Lord God omnipotent rules over all. If God could control Behemoth and Leviathan and could bring out of the chaos a universe of order and meaning, that same God could be trusted in Job's affairs.

Job begins to see not the God of popular theology of his day but God as God really is, infinitely greater in every way than Job had imagined. Job does not know all of life's answers, but he knows the God who has all things under loving care. Job learned that the just shall live by faith, and he was now ready to live, not by his own integrity and righteousness but by faith in the eternal purposes of God. He found that what he needed was not answers to his questions but trust in God.

Continuous study of Scripture led me to the Gospel accounts of Jesus's life and ministry—Matthew, Mark, Luke, and John. These writers reported that with the coming of Jesus, God fully entered human history. He was no longer "up there" but "down here." Jesus took residency in the body of a human being on earth. He became subject to the physical laws and limitations of a person. Therefore, we gain a clue about how God feels about human pain when we look at Jesus's experiences and responses to suffering.

Jesus knew what suffering was all about, not just because of his perfect knowledge but also from his experiences. The Gospels picture Jesus experiencing life's ordinary pressures, difficulties, and hurts. John records how Jesus became weary and thirsty (John 4:6). Mark records Jesus' grief over the hardness of people's hearts (Mark: 3:5). John helps us learn of Jesus' sadness when Lazarus died (John 11:35). Mark also records Jesus' feeling about his coming death: "My soul is deeply grieved, to the point of death" (14:34a). One might imagine that throughout Jesus' lifetime, he experienced such occurrences as the common cold, the stomach virus, the sore throat, the nagging headache, and other common human illnesses. More than likely, when he was a boy he experienced bruises and cuts as other children did. The God in whom we trust knows what suffering is all about because of the incarnation.

From the beginning to the end of Jesus' public, earthly ministry, he knew the pain of being rejected and misunderstood. Even his best friends, family, and nation misunderstood his mission and treated him unfairly. Soon after the beginning of his ministry, enemies of Jesus attempted to kill him. The devil also tempted him to live life his way and not the way of the heavenly Father. Scorn, disdain, and rejection lingered in Jesus' mind from his baptism to his ascension, and being rejected has to be one of the worst emotions a person can face. Jesus did fit the prophetic description of a person "despised and abandoned by men, A man of great pain and familiar with sickness" (Isaiah 53:3a).

In the last week of Jesus' earthly existence, his pain moved to a greater level. He knew that he was going to die, and the Gospel writers pictured him with a sense of dread over the coming event. While Jesus prayed in the Garden of Gethsemane, he was arrested by Roman soldiers. They took him to a Roman civil trial, and the Roman court turned him over to the Jewish court. In his trials, he was falsely accused. He was abandoned by his friends and followers, and he suffered the pain of rejection, denial, and betrayal of those close to him. Even in Jesus' dying hour on the cross, he felt rejected by his heavenly Father, crying out, "MY GOD, MY GOD, WHY HAVE YOU FORSAKEN ME?" (Matthew 27:46b).

The final experience of Jesus being led to his death reflects intense physical agony and emotional distress. This final experience of death, ultimately unfathomable to us, means infinite, cosmic agony beyond the knowledge of any of us on earth. The ultimate suffering is the loss of love.

There is nothing more difficult than the loss of family relationships. God knows what it is like to suffer because God suffered in the most severe way possible. Jesus' actual suffering was not described in detail by the Gospel writers, but in his book *The Crucifixion and Death of a Man Called Jesus*, Dr. David Ball seeks to reconstruct possible medical aspects of a slow execution by crucifixion, describing the intense physical agony that crucifixion caused. The nails in Jesus' hands crushed nerves and caused horrendous hurt. Inhalation and exhalation became quite difficult the longer he hung on the cross.[4]

After Jesus left earth and ascended back to heaven with the Father, his followers continued to suffer as he did. The hurt came from normal life experiences and as a result of their commitment to Christ. One of the most prominent sufferers for Christ was Paul. Several times in the letter known as 2 Corinthians, Paul gave an account of his personal afflictions (2 Corinthians 1:8–10; 4:8–12; 11:21–23; 12:5–10). These disclosures reflect a wide range of physical, emotional, and spiritual hardships. The experiences of Paul included hunger, imprisonment, betrayal, and close calls from shipwreck, beatings, stoning, and robbers. In addition to these problems, he suffered emotional distress over the care of the churches.

How did Paul cope with hardships and pain? He gave us a clue in his Corinthian correspondence: "For we do not want you to be unaware, brothers and sisters, of our affliction which occurred in Asia, that we were burdened excessively, beyond our strength, so that we despaired even of life. Indeed, we had the sentence of death within ourselves so that we would not trust in ourselves, but in God who raises the dead" (2 Corinthians 1:8–9). Paul coped with all of his suffering by trusting in God's strength for him, looking beyond himself to cope with life's hardships: "I can do all things through Him who strengthens me" (Philippians 4:13). Paul did not feel that he was smart enough or strong enough to cope with his circumstances; he had to seek a higher power and a richer wisdom. He found that he could get through tough times with God's help.

Paul called for readers to trust God's sovereign rule of life. What we do is thank God for whatever God is going to do with our request. God has the eternal perspective about our life situations and can see all things working together for our good and for God's glory. In our practice of trusting God, we will eventually come to that perspective. I did.

These biblical references gave me profound insight into pain and suffering. The Bible has a purpose: it is to help us hear God speak. The Bible becomes the voice of God when we open our lives to the Holy Spirit who inspired the Bible. In his hymn about Scripture, Martin Luther wrote, "Beyond the sacred page I seek thee Lord." The Bible helped me hear the word of God. Instead of just academic exercises of reading and studying these Bible passages, they became God speaking informatively and practically to me.

The continued search for resources on pain and suffering led me to meaningful books on the subject. Over three decades ago, I read Harold S. Kushner's bestselling classic titled *When Bad Things Happen to Good People*.[5] Kushner's three-year-old son suffered from progeria, a rapid aging disease. He lived only to his early teens. As Kushner watched his son hurt, he confronted head-on the difficult problem of an innocent person suffering. He learned to accept God's love, but he did question God's power. He said that God wanted to help people who suffered, but God lacked the power to do so. Many people relate to Kushner's idea of bad things happening to God's people. But many readers of the book, including myself, disagree with Kushner's view about God's power. Elie Wiesel had a perceptive comment on the God portrayed by Rabbi Kushner: "If that's who God is, I think he ought to resign and let someone more competent take his place."[6]

I found help in books by three other authors—C. S. Lewis, Philip Yancey, and Timothy Keller. The first book I read after my "aha" moment in Dayton, Ohio, was C. S. Lewis's book *The Problem of Pain*.[7] He addressed the question, "If God is good and all-powerful, why does he allow his creatures to suffer such pain?" Lewis came to the conclusion that God holds good and pain in paradox. He probably wrote on the subject of pain because of his personal questions about pain. His mother died when he was a boy. His father abandoned him. He experienced rejection from his colleagues at Oxford. He later grieved greatly over the death of his wife. In *The Problem of Pain*, he seeks to understand how a loving, good, and powerful God can coexist with pain and suffering. Lewis felt that the presence of pain did not negate the existence of an all-powerful, all-loving God; rather, he felt that God's presence gave him help and hope amid his pain.

In his book titled *Where Is God When It Hurts?* Philip Yancey wrote about the tough problem of pain from an academic and practical perspective. Yancey felt that pain was more than a theoretical problem and closer to a relational and theological problem. Many people want to love and relate to God, but they have a hard time with their tears. They have deep feelings of hurt. So in his book, Yancey deals more with the idea of coping with pain than the task of explaining it. He thinks people in pain need love. Wounded people need a God who loves them and gives them hope. He feels that people who have been broken and helped by God can become a help to other hurting people.

Several years after my pilgrimage with pain started, Timothy Keller wrote his book titled *Walking with God through Pain and Suffering*.[8] When I read this book, I wished that I had possessed it at the beginning of my journey. It helped and continues to help me greatly. Keller used the biblical metaphors of walking for the journey of life and the fiery furnace as a traveler's encounter with pain and suffering. He offered a broader spectrum on pain and suffering than any book I had ever read, dividing the book into three distinctive parts. In the first part he notes the universal phenomenon of human suffering. He shares the various ways that culture, religion, and eras in history sought to help suffering people. This first part is rather philosophical with a lot of scholarship. In this section Keller tackles the classic problem of evil. He warns readers that this first section might be too abstract for a person in pain.

In the second part of the book, Keller moves away from the philosophical realm and examines what the Bible teaches about suffering. He shares the common ways people handle suffering by avoidance, denial, and despair. These ways represent common wastes of suffering. With his biblical teaching, Keller moves into a more productive result of pain. He writes that sufferers need to face hardships realistically and seek help from God. These trials are the fires God uses to mold character.

The third part of Keller's book is practical. He writes about strategies for connecting to God while walking through pain and suffering. He does not promise that all suffering will lead to full resolution or a happy ending in this life, but he includes first-person stories about how people of faith have dealt with varieties of hurt and pain and found help and profit. These testimonies mainly relate how God walked with them through the trials of life. The philosophical and theological sections of Keller's book educated me to a greater awareness of pain and how people of other cultures have coped with it. But Keller's third section helped me the most. In these six chapters, he offered practical therapy for my struggle with pain.

My journey continued with the use of another resource: the observation of pain in other travelers through life. Just opening my eyes to the suffering of others added to my knowledge. The daily news on television brought to my attention the many hurts happening to other people—reports of murders, mass killings, terrorist activities, rape, child abuse. Every hour five children throughout the world die from abuse and violence.[9] I heard about deaths from traffic accidents, illnesses, and strange, unexpected tragedies; television pictures reported the results of tsunamis, tornadoes, hurricanes, volcanoes, and floods. In addition to seeing and hearing about the hurt done to other people, I became aware of self-inflicted pain as reports of suicides came to my attention. These occurrences bought to my mind the inward emotional trauma these people faced before they took their lives and the enormous hurt suicide brought to their family and friends. The more I opened my eyes to life's happenings, the more I became aware that I live in a world full of enormous pain.

In *Regarding the Pain of Others*, Susan Sontag published graphic pictures of pain with her photographs of war and violence.[10] These spectacles of suffering greatly affected me. Sontag included pictures of the disasters of several wars in the world, the lynching of Black people in the South, and Nazi concentration camps. She included visual images of violence in Bosnia, Sierra Leone, Palestine, and New York City on September 11, 2001. Her images moved me from mere personal observation to empathetic feelings about human hurt.

All along my journey of studying Scripture, reading books, and observing the pain of others, I have made an intentional attempt to engage in personal conversations with people in pain. I want to understand and feel their thoughts and emotions. Taking the time to talk with wounded travelers has created another great resource in my search for information on pain and suffering. Numerous occasions have offered opportunities to listen. I have intentionally visited people in hospitals, hospices, rest homes, and rehabilitation centers. When I served as an interim pastor in churches, people came to me for counseling. Oddly enough, even casual encounters with people brought conversations about joy, sorrow, agonies, ecstasies, doubts, and affirmations.

In his book *The Awesome Power of the Listening Ear*, John Drakeford helped me with the conversational element of my pilgrimage.[11] He taught me that listening differs from hearing. The act of hearing involves a basic physical function, while listening involves an active process where a person chooses to focus and assign meaning to what is being heard. Listening happens as a skill or a discipline. In my personal conversations with people in pain, I began to restrict my talking. I sought to keep my mind on what people were saying. I chose not to interrupt with interpretations or instructions. I heard the words of others and sought to determine what they meant by their words. As I listened, I practiced empathetic imagination—the capacity in a large measure to understand what a person is experiencing without having had that experience.

People in pain have given me enormous insights about their hurts and feelings, and their words have taught me more about the dynamics of pain. I learned that many of the sufferers had the same feelings I had. Oddly enough, after I listened for a while, the people in pain often said, "Thanks for your help." I realized I did not give them much advice or make many evaluations. I just listened. Listening was the gift I gave to them, and from their conversations about their hurt, help is the gift I received in return.

Biblical revelation, academic readings, personal observations, and intentional and casual conversations were all important resources that furnished abundant help for my pilgrimage. These resources moved me from preoccupation with my own hurt to the thoughts and feelings of others about hurt. I continue to use all four resources because the journey has not ended. I constantly continue to learn. Thank God I began an intentional journey to take time for my pain.

### Notes

[1] Leonard Griffith, *God in Man's Experience: The Activity of God in the Psalms* (Waco, TX: Word Books, 1968), 13.

[2] Hermann Gunkel, *The Psalms: A Form-Critical Introduction* (Philadelphia: Fortress Press, 1967).

[3] Philip Yancey, *Where Is God When It Hurts?* (Grand Rapids: Zondervan Publishing House, 1990), i.

[4] David Ball, *The Crucifixion and Death of a Man Called Jesus* (Bloomington, IN: Cross Books, 2009).

[5] Harold Kushner, *When Bad Things Happen to Good People* (1981; repr., New York: Anchor Books, 2004).

[6] Quoted in Yancey, *Where Is God When It Hurts?* 105.

⁷ C. S. Lewis, *The Problem of Pain* (New York: Harper Collins Books, 1940).

⁸ Timothy Keller, *Walking with God Through Pain and Suffering* (New York: Penguin Books, 2013).

⁹ Ibid., 1.

¹⁰ Susan Sontag, *Regarding the Pain of Others* (New York: Picador Farrar, Straus and Giroux, 2003).

¹¹ John Drakeford, *The Awesome Power of the Listening Ear* (Nashville: Broadman Press, 1967).

# Chapter 3

# Searching for a Cause

Inquiring minds want to know what causes tragic events to happen. Why did the airplane crash immediately after takeoff? What caused the limousine accident that killed twenty people? The United States government has an investigation organization designed to search for reasons behind aviation accidents, automobile crashes, railroad accidents, and ship disasters. Members of the National Transportation Board travel to the site of a particular accident and search for evidence that could give a hint about the possible cause.

Humans also explore other serious questions of a more personal nature. What caused an eleven-year-old boy to have brain cancer? What caused my young wife to be stricken with Alzheimer's? Where can I find the reason for my failed marriage? What really caused me to lose my job? Why did my husband die so quickly and so young? What caused my repeated occurrences of cancer? Searching for the cause of diseases, sicknesses, and handicaps never seems to stop. The search continues, and many times it is futile.

Two other prominent questions have been asked for ages. The first question is one of origins. What caused the heavens and the earth to form, and how did human beings originate? The second question centers on evil, suffering, and pain. When did suffering and pain begin, and why does human suffering happen? Numerous civilizations have searched for the cause of the universe, earth, and human beings. Thousands of years ago, the ancient Babylonians and Egyptians had accounts of the beginning of creation, including the origin of the earth and the human species. The Babylonian account of creation was known as *Enuma Elish*. The Egyptians had a lengthy account of beginnings dating back to 2400–2300 BC. Both of these ancient creation accounts contain lengthy, complicated stories that portray creation's dawn in terms of many pagan deities. Centuries have passed since the Babylonian and Egyptian accounts, but the search for the origin of the universe, the earth, and human beings has not stopped. Scientists have been working for years to solve the mystery of the beginning of the world and of human life.

The second question about the cause of suffering and pain has also been asked for centuries. It continues to be asked. Philosophers stumble over answers to that question, and some have rejected the existence of God because of the presence of pain and suffering. C. E. M. Joad, Bertrand Russell, and Voltaire address the presence of pain as a strong argument against the religious views of the universe. The presence of pain does represent a profound riddle, and the philosopher's approach to the subject sometimes takes the form of abstract reasoning. But most of the problems of pain and suffering cannot be answered with mental gymnastics.

So where else can we go to search for the cause of our world's origins and the presence of pain and suffering? I have chosen to read carefully the account of creation in Genesis, which has greatly enlightened me about the source of creation and has also surprised me with its teachings on the cause of pain and suffering. The book of Genesis derives its name from a word meaning "birth or origin." The Hebrews call this first book (Genesis) by its first word—*bere'shith*—which translates to "in the beginning." The first four chapters of Genesis afford reasonable answers to searches for the origins of a good world and the reason for an evil presence that perpetuates pain and suffering within that world.

Genesis has the qualities of a narration. It is a continuous story of events and experiences. In my search for causes of creation and pain, I have noticed the sequential happenings recorded in Genesis. There are four episodes in Genesis 1–4, and they are as follows: the source of creation (1:1–2:25), the beginning of suffering (3:1–7), the spread of pain and suffering (3:8–24), and the provocation of hurts on other human beings (4:1–24). The first narrative opens our minds to the origin and presence of a good world and perfect human beings. The second episode introduces readers to the human Fall. The third episode goes on to tell us how the Fall led to the subjects of agony of *Paradise Lost* and the theme of *Paradise Regained* in episodes three and four. Now, let's begin the reading of the narrative and search for causes of various occurrences.

The first episode opens with the beginning of creation (1:1–2:25). The phrase "in the beginning" signals the cause of heaven and earth. The writer then records the appearance of God in the creation: "In the beginning

God" (1:1a). These words indicate that God started the heavens and the earth and that nothing existed before God created it. God has no beginning or end. God is the eternal now. The narrator further indicates that God created the heavens and the earth from nothing: "In the beginning God created." The word "created" was only used for God, and the writer indicates that God created everything with the inclusive statement "the heavens and the earth" (1:1b). Everything below, above, and between is the handiwork of God.[1]

The God-centeredness of creation stands out prominently throughout the creation episode. God is the subject of nearly every verb in chapter 1. The statement "God said" occurs ten times. God's evaluation of creation with the word "good" appears seven times, and "very good" appears one time. The name "God" appears forty-six times in Genesis 1:1–2:3, and it comes from the Hebrew noun *Elohim*, the root of which means "strength" and "power." The message is clear that God has the strength and power to make the heavens and the earth. God is before all, back of all, and above all.

The creation narrative in Genesis speaks of the heavens and the earth as an empty and undeveloped state: "And the earth was a formless and desolate emptiness, and darkness was over the surface of the deep" (1:2a). Material seems to have had an elemental form, and from it God brought forth an ordered existence. The narrator records in verses 1 and 2 how God created the material, and in verses 3 through 25 the writer tells how God shaped things out of this material.[2]

The creation account indicates the presence of God in the shaping of heaven and earth: "and the Spirit of God was hovering over the surface of the waters" (1:2b). These words communicate that God is the Creator, Sustainer, and Shaper of creation. God knew what God was doing and controlled what was happening. From the creation account, readers also see that God created by God's word. God spoke and creation happened, saying, "let there be…," and light, firmament, plants, stars, fish, birds, animals, and human beings came into existence. God's word expressed what God wanted, and what happened came as a result of that word.

One of the striking features of Genesis 1 is its pattern. The story is structured around the theme of one week of six days leading to a seventh. The repetitive refrain—"there was evening and there was morning"—moves the story along. The gradually increasing complexity of what God created, beginning with formless material and ending with human beings, gives readers a deep sense of order in creation. First, "the earth was a formless and desolate emptiness" (1:2a). The words "formless" and "desolate" come from a play on two Hebrew words similar in sound. The word "formless" (*tohu*) means that the material God had not created had no shape or form. The word "desolate" or "void" (*bohu*) means that the creation did not have structure. From the formless and void mass, God brought shape.

The writer then tells of the three days of separation. On day one, God separated the light from the darkness. The readers can see a parallel between this first separation and that of day four, in which God makes the light-bearers, the sun and the moon, to rule over the day and the night (1:4, 16–18). On day two, God separated the waters of the firmament of the heavens from the waters under the heavens. This separation can be seen in parallel with day five, in which God makes birds to fly across the heavens and sea monsters and fish to swim in the seas (1:7, 20). On day three, God separated the dry land from the seas and gave fertile vegetation. This can be seen in parallel with day six, in which God makes animals, domestic and wild, to inhabit the earth. God also makes human beings, male and female, to have dominion over all other living creatures. The narrative relates form coming from formlessness. These three separations disclose the origin of order and design. Stage by stage, readers see God changing disorder into order, chaos into cosmos.[3]

Following the sixth day, God brought forth the seventh day. God's creation was finished. "And so the heavens and the earth were completed, and all their heavenly lights" (2:1). "Then God blessed the seventh day and sanctified it" (2:3a). The seventh day was set apart from the ordinary and common activity and put to holy use with special attention to God: "on it He rested from all His work which God had created and made" (2:3b). The term "rest" does not refer to relaxation after an exhausting time of work; rather, it describes the enjoyment of what God had made.[4]

Throughout the creation process, God made evaluations. Five times God described the work as "good" (1:10, 12, 18, 21, and 25). God's evaluation reached a crescendo with the statement, "And God saw all that He had made, and behold, it was very good" (1:31a). The terms "good" and "very good" mean that all of God's creation had met God's intentions. It was a beautiful, idyllic creation. No pain or suffering existed.

The writer of Genesis links a second account of creation (2:4–25) with the first account (1:1–2:3). In the second account, the writer tells how

God developed what was said about creation in the first account. The second account means a fuller development of the story of creation, and it contains noticeable differences compared with the first. Probably the most noticeable change is the name of God. The writer changes from "God" to "the LORD God" in the second account. The name "LORD God" discloses that the transcendent God, the Creator, is also intimately involved in fellowship with the man and woman that God made. This name "LORD God" comes from the covenant name *Yahweh* in Hebrew. The focus of interest from Genesis 2:4 onward is no longer the cosmic perspective of the One who made all things; it shifts to the intimacy of fellowship with the One who calls man and woman by name.

Notice the fuller development early in the second account of creation: "Then the LORD God formed the man of dust from the ground, and breathed into his nostrils the breath of life; and man became a living person" (2:7). The expressions "formed" and "breathed" represent an equivalent of the expression "image of God" in chapter 1. The breath of God means that human beings get the gift of life from God. Humans have a nature or spark in them that makes them kin or patterned after the divine. The phrase "living person" refers to the principle of life in all living organisms.

An important event happened when God planted a garden: "The LORD God planted a garden toward the east, in Eden; and there He placed the man whom He had formed" (2:8). The garden was located at the center of the earth, and in it God planted all kinds of trees that represented the garden's majestic beauty and provided food and shelter for living creatures. There God also planted the tree of life (2:15–17) and the tree of knowledge of good and evil. The word garden (*eden*) can be translated as "garden of delight" or "paradise." Thus, the purpose of the story is to indicate that humans were created by God to dwell in happiness and idealism in this paradisiacal existence, which meant fellowship with God and enjoyment of all that God had created.

The creation story continues with more insight about the garden. God assigned Adam to "cultivate and tend" the garden (2:15). From the beginning, God charged humanity with responsible work. In addition, God gave two specific commandments, one of permission and the other of prohibition. In the first God generously permitted the human access to all the trees, including the tree of life. In the second, God prohibited the human from eating of the tree of the knowledge of good and evil. To disobey this second commandment meant the penalty of death.

A marvelous scene of the creation narrative appears after citing that the man was alone in the garden: "Then the LORD God said, 'It is not good for the man to be alone; I will make him a helper suitable for him'" (2:18). The word "suitable" suggested a person significantly different from Adam, yet one who was of the same essence and on the same level with him. The narrator relates how God brought animals to see if any of them could be a helper to Adam. None of the animals qualified (see 2:19–20). God then caused a deep sleep to fall upon the man, taking one of his ribs and closing the flesh where it was opened. These details teach us that no other living creature could ever become woman's rival in serving as man's helper, counterpart, and intimate companion.

When the man saw the woman for the first time, he exclaimed ecstatically that she was "bone of my bones and flesh of my flesh" (verse 23). She was the one God had designed for a bonded relationship and meaningful companionship. The writer states that both the man and the woman were naked, but they were not ashamed. These humans possessed complete innocence. They were not marked by disorder or hampered by shame. The creation episode closes with the man and the woman in paradise in an idyllic relationship. God is wonderful! God created a perfect world, putting man and woman in a garden to enjoy a perfect relationship. Life does not get any better than that. At least one of our questions receives an answer: "What is the source of creation and the human race?" The answer is simple yet profound. God created the world and all that is in it.

So far in the Genesis story recorded in chapters 1 and 2, we have had a pleasant, enjoyable read. Maybe the reading of this biblical material has prompted a question from the reader: "Why has a lengthy discussion on creation been included in a book on pain and suffering?" Pain, hurt, evil, and suffering do not appear in Genesis 1 and 2. My purpose in including the creation narrative has been to show how God did not originally intend humans to experience pain and suffering. The creation story answers our question: God is not responsible for pain and suffering. God created a good world with idyllic relationships. In our search for the source of the created universe, earth, and human life, we have found the answer in Genesis 1 and 2. To search for the cause of pain and suffering, we must keep reading and studying Genesis beyond chapter 2.

The story of human beings takes a drastic turn in Genesis 3, where it continues with a scene in the garden. A new actor appears in the scene. It is a serpent. "Now the serpent was more cunning than any animal of the field which the LORD God had made" (3:1). He had not been content to live outside the garden and instead contrived an entry into it. The story does not focus on the serpent per se but on the human response to the possibilities the serpent presents. The serpent represented anything in God's creation that could present options to human beings, the choice of which could seduce them away from God. The serpent knew what the woman really wanted. She wanted to eat of that tree of knowledge and know good and evil. She really wanted to be like God.

The serpent initiated a conversation with Eve—a theological dialogue that readers of the Genesis story overhear. The serpent asked Eve about God's prohibition to the man and the woman, questioning the amount of freedom God had given human beings. The question focused on God as the serpent asked, "Have I got this straight? Did God really say that you were not to eat of any tree?" Eve responded to the serpent's questions. She stated that all trees were available to her and to her husband except the tree in the middle of the garden. To eat from that tree would incur the penalty of death, Eve said. They were not even to touch that tree (she added this detail to God's original prohibition). The serpent openly challenged this and pointed out that to eat from that tree would confer upon the couple similarity to God. The serpent said to Eve, "For God knows that on the day you eat from it your eyes will be opened, and you will become like God, knowing good and evil" (3:5). The serpent claimed that God knew the man and the woman would become like God and thus needlessly threatened them with death. The serpent planted in Eve's mind that she could be the master of her fate and the captain of her soul. The serpent led Eve to doubt the goodness of God, the integrity of God, and the truth of the word of God.

Eve gazed at the forbidden tree. She had never examined it closely. Now, she saw that the tree was good to eat, attractive to handle, and enlightening to her mind (see 3:6a). She reached for the fruit on the tree. She enjoyed the fruit and quickly shared it with Adam. The narrator of the story put his finger on the basic desire of human beings—the desire to acknowledge no one as Lord but yourself. Both Adam and Even wanted to be equal with God, and they overstepped their creaturehood when they disobeyed God's command.

The story of the human race changed with that decision: "she took some of its fruit and ate; and she also gave some to her husband with her, and he ate" (3:6b). This action of the couple is known as the Fall. It was a fall because the couple moved away from the responsible decision concerning their destiny and let their own desire dominate them. Something went wrong after the couple's disobedience to God. Life became different for them. Since then, humans have never been what God intended them to be. They have failed to realize God's purpose. They continually refuse to admit their creaturehood and submit to the will of God.

The rest of the story in Genesis 3 deals with the outcome of the couple's venture. The first change came when Adam and Eve noticed that they were naked. Something had shifted within the human psyche. "Then the eyes of both of them were opened, and they knew that they were naked" (3:7a). They tried to cover themselves with fig leaves. This was not the situation in the idyllic state of creation, when "the man and his wife were both naked, but they were not ashamed" (2:25). The expression "naked and ashamed" underscored the pressure of uneasiness with themselves. It meant not only being uncomfortable with one's self but also being uncomfortable with others. The pressure of shame introduced the presence of pain within human feelings.

Human awareness of nakedness resulted in the consequence of alienation from God. Formerly, Adam and Eve lived in a wholesome experience of fellowship with God. But now they became aware that something had happened. Instead of maintaining openness with God, they wanted to hide. When the couple heard the sound of the LORD God in the garden, they hid among the trees. The guilt made them ashamed and fearful of being in God's presence. The clothing they made failed to provide them sufficient confidence to meet God.

After encountering Adam and Eve, God spoke of the consequences of the Fall on the serpent and the ground: "Because you have done this, Cursed are you more than all the livestock, And more than any animal of the field; On your belly shall you go, And dust shall you eat All the days of your life" (Genesis 3:14). The word "curse" expressed God's judgment, which was an indication of coming misfortunes. The blessings were reversed. The joyous presence of an idyllic creation became a dirge, a shadow that fell over all things.

God continues with the sentencing, acting as a judge. Turning again to the serpent, God says, "And I will make enemies Of you and the woman, And of your offspring and her Descendant; He shall bruise you on the head, And you shall bruise Him on the heel" (Genesis 3:15). The serpent received a curse, becoming isolated from the community of animals. In the future it would move on its belly and eat dust. This judgment signified humiliation and degradation. God placed enmity between the serpent and the woman and between the offspring of both. This judgment represented a lifelong struggle between good and evil. The "head" and the "heel" were the targets against each other. Striking the head of the serpent would likely prove decisive and would give hope to humans about the ultimate defeat of evil.

After speaking words of judgment to the serpent, God spoke to the woman. "To the woman he said, 'I will greatly multiply Your pain in childbirth. In pain you shall deliver children; Yet your desire will be for your husband'" (3:16). The woman's sentence involved painful and difficult childbirth. Rebellion against God disrupted the harmony of God's creation. The Fall is a dimension of human experience that is always present in everyone, namely that we who have been created for fellowship with God repudiate it continually. The Fall is not just about Adam and Eve; it is about all people. This punishment and pain perverted what God had intended.

God's next pronouncement of punishment came to the man. He acted as one with the woman in eating the forbidden fruit. He agreed with the woman in disobeying God and eating from the tree of knowledge. God declared that the ground, the source of life-giving food, was cursed because of the man's act. The land became subject to a variety of plagues. Thorns and thistles would rob the soil of moisture and nutrients and choke out the fruit-bearing plants. Consequently, the man would experience pain in working the ground.

The narrator of Genesis wrote words of God banishing Adam and Eve from the garden, stationing the cherubim and the flaming sword to guard its entrance. The curse, the disruption, the toil, and the banishment are all consequences stemming from God's word recorded in 2:17: "on the day that you eat from it [the tree of knowledge] you will certainly die."

Death meant more than the physical cessation of life. Death meant a change. This change led to psychological dysfunction, theological estrangement, sociological alienation, and cosmological disruption. Genesis 1 and 2 show us a world without pain and suffering and depict humankind placed within that world. Genesis 3 records the spiritual death initiated by human choice.

Eating the forbidden fruit did not give the couple the power of being like God. Rather, they began to exist outside the garden with a susceptibility to physical and emotional weaknesses. The Fall led to frail human beings becoming subject to sickness, disease, and accidents. These experiences lead to pain, suffering, and even death. Reminders throughout the course of life cause each person to confess, "I am not God. I am a human being with many frailties."

Numerous factors make us aware of our human weaknesses. The experience of aging becomes one of the most prominent signs that our bodies are in a decaying process. Aging causes us to think about the unending cycle of life, which begins with conception, continues after birth with growth, and follows with decline and death. Paul wrote in Romans 8 about the weakness of the human body, "For we know that the whole creation groans and suffers the pains of childbirth together until now" (8:22).

When we age, contrasting feelings come to us. We celebrate growth, development, and survival, but the passing of time brings complaints about aches and pains. Birthdays remind us how fast life moves and how much more perishable we become. Various markers awaken us to signs of aging. One marker for me came in my early forties when I had to wear glasses. The visual problems kept coming with bifocals and later trifocals. Also, skin spots and wrinkles appeared on my skin as I aged. Another marker of my aging came with the loss of my hair. Only recently, the prescription for hearing aids made me aware that I was a "frail child of dust." In her book *Passages*, Gail Sheehy reminds me that I am now in the last passage of my life. I am human, and I cannot stop the aging process. It just gets more pronounced.

Failures in our lives teach us how weak and vulnerable we are. No person is perfect. People fail in educational pursuits, in sporting events, in the workplace, in marriages, and in other interpersonal relationships. No baseball player bats a thousand, and no pitcher throws a no-hitter every game. No matter how hard we try in life pursuits, we sometimes fail.

Paul recognized the possibility of human failure in life: "I do not understand what I am doing; for I am not practicing what I want to do, but I do the very thing I hate" (Romans 7:15).

The greatest failure of any human being comes with disobeying God's clear commands. The best people are susceptible to moral failure. David, who was characterized as a man after God's heart, committed adultery with Uriah's wife Bathsheba. His infidelity led him to murder Uriah so he could marry Bathsheba himself. Later, the prophet Nathan confronted David about his actions. David then cried to the Lord, "Be gracious to me, God" (Psalm 51:1a). No one can have any greater private pain than to disobey the Lord.

Human pain appears not only with physical distresses. It also appears with mental and emotional suffering. God said to Adam and Eve, "You will surely die." As we said previously, death means not only a physical cessation of life but also emotional and mental distresses brought by alienation from God, a dysfunctional self, impaired human relationships, and a disrupted natural order. The human Fall disrupted God's original design for life. It created physical deterioration, damaged emotions, and mental anguish. We now live on a groaning planet bemoaning the conditions of the world and the human race. We lament the frailties that come to mind and body. Human beings introduced "dying" to the planet. It was a departure from God's original design.

Paul commented on humanity's frail condition. "Therefore," he wrote, "we do not lose heart, but though our outer man is decaying, yet our inner man is being renewed day by day" (2 Corinthians 4:16). Paul identified himself with the reality of human mortality. He told the Corinthians that what was happening to him was happening to everyone, speaking of human existence being in a process of decay. He made repeated references to his afflictions, persecutions, and hardships (see 2 Corinthians 1:8–11; 4:7–11). Robert Grant wrote the hymn "O Worship the King." The last stanza depicts the fragile condition of human beings: "Frail children of dust, and feeble as frail, in Thee do we trust nor find Thee to fail." Paul openly embraced the picture of himself as a "frail child of dust."

The Genesis story does not stop with Adam and Eve. It continues in chapter 4. Even though the door is shut to the garden and the cherubim and the sword guard the gate, God allows life to continue in a fallen world outside the garden. The narrator continues the story with the birth of two sons: Cain and Abel. Even though they had the same parents, Cain and Abel differed from each other. Abel was a keeper of sheep, and Cain was a tiller of the ground. Neither one of their occupations were condemned. After the brothers began to prosper, each one presented an offering to God. Cain presented an offering from the field, and Abel brought an offering from the flock. The Lord looked with favor on Abel's offering but not on Cain's. The narrator does not say why God chose Abel's offering over Cain's; one can only conclude by reading the text of Genesis 4 that God responded to the attitudes of the brothers.

In response to the Lord favoring Abel's offering, Cain became angry and his countenance fell. He became despondent, and he was filled with contempt for his brother. His jealousy had to be confronted before it led him to do something terribly wrong. Time passed with Cain's negative attitude toward Abel increasing. One day he met his brother in a field. The biblical writer says nothing about the conversation between the two—only that Cain's jealousy and anger took control of him, and he killed Abel.

After Abel's murder, the Lord asked Cain, "Where is Abel your brother?" Cain sarcastically responded, "I do not know. Am I my brother's keeper?" God then pronounced a punishment upon Cain, cursing him and driving him from the ground that received his brother's blood. God caused Cain to be separated from the support of the land, making him "a wanderer on the earth." Cain complained bitterly about being driven from the land. He feared that anyone he met might kill him. The Lord then put a "sign" on Cain that would prevent anyone from taking his life.

The Genesis story shares more with us about the results of rebellion against God. To be human means to be responsible to God, and it also means to be aware of our inner attitudes and external actions. Uncontrolled anger on Cain's part led him to anger, and that anger led him to hurt not only himself but also someone dear to him. Unchecked and uncontrolled inner attitudes can lead to destructive, addictive habits and become a source of pain and suffering. Human beings harm themselves with uncontrolled use of drugs and alcohol. The National Survey on Drug Use and Health in 2014 reported that 467,000 adolescents aged twelve to seventeen were users of non-medical pain relievers.[5] Other addictions such as gambling, pornography, sex, work, and eating harm the lives of people. These facts represent a lot of self-inflicted pain and suffering. The harm of both self and others continues to exist since the Fall.

In many cases, unchecked inner struggles have also led to suicide. According to the CDC's National Center for Health Statistics, 47,511 people took their own lives in 2019.[6] Think of the inward pain these people held before their self-destructive act, and consider the great pain felt by their family members and friends. Relatives search for the reason or reasons for the suicidal act, but often the inner struggles of a person who commits suicide never surface. Loved ones are left to suffer painful grief, and sometimes anger, about a mysterious action. Suicide leaves a long trail of pain.

Rebellion against God not only causes people to hurt themselves but also causes them to harm other people. Think of the wars fought throughout human history. Ponder the number of soldiers and civilians killed because of human conflict. Countries, citizens, and other groups fight because they want their way. The death and the wounding of soldiers in wars has brought lifelong pain to family members. During my lifetime, America has been in conflict with Japan, Germany, Korea, Vietnam, Iraq, and Afghanistan. I researched the number of deaths these clashes produced, and I was astounded. Over the past eight decades, Americans and America's enemies have experienced incredible pain. Human conflict started with Cain and Abel, and it has only intensified through the years.

While thinking about pain inflicted by other people, I have also thought about crime-related death. The action of Cain continues to be repeated. In the United States, there were a total of 17,284 murders in 2017. Psychologists report that grief over a loved one's murder brings many emotional dynamics that are difficult to master. In addition to murder, mass shootings over the past twenty years have caused great grief. Between 2017 and 2021, mass shootings have left 310 people dead and 646 wounded.[7] These events have brought intense pain. I once lived only a few miles away from one school shooting. I had a difficult time understanding that kind of action. The day after the shooting, I had coffee with one of my colleagues. I asked him, "What causes a person to do such a thing?" He responded, "Harold, remember the Fall and Cain."

Human beings also hurt other human beings with rape, incest, and sexual harassment. Victims of these abuses suffer greatly the moment the hurt happens. But the aggressor's actions linger for a long time with the victims, in most cases for a lifetime. In 2015, there were 90,185 rapes in America according to statistics from law enforcement.[8] Of course, this number only represents the reported cases. Jack Finegan wrote, "The result of the fall is that fallen man is up against evil that is too much for him."⁹

Pain and suffering have multiplied greatly on earth since the Fall, and they continue to increase. The source seems to be the abuse of human freedom. We cannot blame the Fall on God, for God is good and wants what is good for creation. We cannot blame the fall on the serpent, for it simply faced Adam and Eve with the question of their responsibility. The fault for the Fall is within us. We have found the enemy, and it is us.

God is not pleased with what happened to creation. God's story continues from Genesis to Revelation. It contains the plan for God to restore creation to its original state of perfection. Between the Fall and God's future restoration, civilization struggles with the results of *Paradise Lost* and looks forward to the promise of *Paradise Restored*. It will be an existence of no more pain, suffering, or death.

### Notes

¹ Ralph Elliot, *The Message of Genesis* (Nashville: Broadman Press, 1961), 29–30.

² Ibid., 31–32.

³ Derek Kidner, "Genesis: An Introduction and Commentary," in *The Old Testament Commentaries*, ed. D. J. Wiseman (Downer's Grove, IL: InterVarsity Press, 1967), 44–52.

⁴ Ibid., 53.

⁵ "Behavioral Health Trends in the United States," September 2015, https://www.samhsa.gov/data/report/behavioral-health-trends-united-states-results-2014-national-survey-drug-use-and-health.

⁶ American Foundation for Suicide Prevention, February 9, 2021, afsp.org.

⁷ "41 Years of Mass Shootings in the United States in One Chart," *TIME*, updated April 16, 2021, https://time.com/4965022/deadliest-mass-shooting-us-history/.

⁸ "Rape Cases Increased the Second Year in a Row," n.d., https://www.bjs.ojp.gov.

⁹ Jack Finegan, *In the Beginning: A Journey through Genesis* (New York: Harper and Brothers Publishers, 1962), 25.

## Chapter 4

# Noticeable Symptoms

Life experiences bring many types of suffering, and these hurtful episodes cause a great range of human responses. One set of symptoms does not fit every hurtful encounter; different crises produce different symptoms. Though different kinds of suffering bring distinct symptoms, a kinship of hurt exists. Experience forbids us to use one single template to match all suffering with specific pains. Just as there is not one set of symptoms for all suffering, there is not one set of practical steps to help with hurt.

Pain comes from many sources and produces many dynamics of hurt. It is crucial to recognize the remarkable variety of human crises. It is also important to understand that different people experience pain with unique temperaments and distinct feelings. In her book *Waiting for God*, Simone Weil identifies two general categories of pain: an internal hurt and an external hurt.[1] Weil makes a distinction between affliction, which is the internal experience of pain and suffering, and suffering in the external circumstances of the world.

Recognizing the variety of suffering and the variety of responses to different hurts helps us with our pilgrimage with pain. Many people's suffering comes from situations that produce internal feelings of pain, noticeable primarily to the sufferer but not so much to the observer. Think of a few examples of internal pain. A woman hurts because a driver veered into her traffic lane, and the resulting crash killed him. The woman suffers the private pain of seeing the crash, living with the results, and replaying how she could have prevented the accident. More than likely, her internal pain will linger with her for a lifetime. Her family and friends sympathize with her, but no one can observe and know her private pain.

Or maybe a wife has an unexpected conversation with her husband of over twenty years. He says, "I am no longer in love with you; I have found another person with whom to live my life. I want a divorce."

Shock, surprise, and disbelief comes to the wife. Hurt descends immediately into the depths of her being. As the days and years pass, she continues to struggle with being rejected. She has to adjust to being a single mother. She has to work to supplement her income. She suffers in silence over the loss of a companion and the breakup of her family. Her friends know that she is hurting, but there is no way they can feel the intensity of her feelings. Countless people have pain like this deep within their being.

Then, as Weil writes, there are the hurts that come from external circumstances life brings. Think of some examples where external life situations bring unexplainable pain. Two parents anticipate the birth of their first child, and a sonogram shows that it will be a girl. They prepare her room and buy her baby clothes. But when the baby is born, she has a brain disorder that affects her motor skills and later her speaking ability. Her parents struggle to make life comfortable and enjoyable for her; as they watch her struggle with life issues, they continue to love and help her. The daughter suffers for eighteen years from an external invasion that occurred when she was within the womb. At the age of eighteen she dies, and the parents grieve greatly over her passing.

All of us hurt from life's external circumstances, and all of us will have inevitable feelings of pain and sorrow. I have experienced lots of internal and external pain. Friends have asked me, "What pain hurt the most, the divorce (internal) or the cancer (external)?" My only answer was, and continues to be, "I hurt, and that's all I can say. I hurt." Each crisis experience in my life hurt me. I have never thought about which painful experience hurt the worst. Internal and external pain do not have different groups of symptoms. Internal pain shows external signs; external pain brings internal hurts. Based on my personal experiences with internal and external pain, I have observed five noticeable symptoms.

These five symptoms did not come to me in any particular order. All of the symptoms seemed to be present in any hurtful circumstance. The first noticeable sign of my pain could be labeled as self-absorption. Pain caused me to be preoccupied with myself. Pain has the ability to pull us down into ourselves so that we hardly notice what is happening in our lives and in the lives of others. I had a hard time thinking of anyone else or anything else when I was in pain. The pain within me took center stage. Suffering seemed to make me think that my needs were the only solid, real thing in life.

This self-absorption makes a person unable to give, receive, or feel love. There is numbness inside them. In *The Lord of the Rings*, J. R. R. Tolkien wrote that the effect of the One Ring was to magnify the ego. So when Samwise put on the Ring, all things around him became vague. He existed in a grey, hazy world, alone, like a small black rock, with a concentrated fixation on what happened to him.[2] Similarly, Simon Weil wrote that when in pain, one may be unable to get outside of oneself and think of, serve, or love others. She also wrote that one may experience the loss of any sense of God: "Affliction makes God appear to be absent for a time, more absent than a dead man, more absent than light in the utter darkness of a cell.... During this time there is nothing to love."[3] When in pain, we may intellectually think and spiritually believe that God loves us, but God's love does not become real to us.

In my deep internal times of pain, I thought incessantly about myself. I thought a lot about what the hurtful circumstance could do to me as a person. I also asked, "What do people think of me now?" When I became a divorced minister, I was filled with feelings that ministry was over for me. I asked, "What does this situation do to my career and my future?" I became preoccupied with my thoughts and with what others thought. My self-absorption became noticeable to many of my close friends. When I saw them, I rarely asked about what was taking place in their lives. I was more interested in telling them about what had happened to me and what was currently happening to me. I told my friends the same sad, hurtful stories over and over again. I am thankful that my friends saw my self-absorption and continued to listen to me, understanding that I was going through a tough time.

My self-absorption also seemed to drive me to a more selfish contact with God. In my prayers I became preoccupied with what I wanted God to do for me. The pronouns "I," "me," "my," "mine" dominated my prayers. In my relational crisis, I prayed earnestly, "Please, Lord, bring my wife back to me." Later, I realized that my request was for my comfort, my career, and my reputation. In my prayers I was not thinking of my wife's interests. During this intense hurtful period, I read James 4:3: "You ask and do not receive, because you ask with the wrong motives, so that you may spend what you request on your pleasures." Also, a friend gave me a book by Max Lucado titled *It's Not about Me*. Lucado reminded me of the simple lesson that being a believer is not about us. He wrote, "When

God looks at the center of the universe, he doesn't look at you."[4] I learned again what I had known earlier in my life: that God is far more interested in our character than in our comforts. Moving gradually away from self-absorption awakened me to significant events taking place around me and to the needs of other people.

A second noticeable symptom of my pain was psychomotor, or psychosomatic, reactions. I began to have physical problems caused by my emotional distress. During the time of my relational crisis, I had many physical problems. My personal physician told me that I was experiencing somatic symptoms because of my mental anguish. My blood pressure began to elevate. My pulse became more rapid. Skin rashes developed on my legs, face, arms, and scalp. My doctor chose not to treat the physical problems. Instead, he worked with my emotional distress. He suggested that I get a good night's sleep, eat three healthy meals per day, and take long, brisk walks. I took his advice, and it helped me get my emotions under control. My physical symptoms improved, and many went away.

A third noticeable symptom of pain was the feeling of helplessness. Observation helped me to see people who could not help themselves. I saw people with birth defects that had left them with the inability to participate in daily life activities that many of us take for granted. One such young woman I encountered needed help eating and moving from place to place. I was told that she was eighteen years old, and she had been in that condition since birth. Though I could not talk with her about her feelings, I could see a person in a helpless condition.

My mother suffered from Alzheimer's disease. A once self-sufficient, strong lady was reduced to weakness both in body and in mind. Her condition necessitated that she be put in a full-time care facility. The kind attendants fed her, took care of her body functions, bathed her, and dressed her. Not only did I see my mother's condition each time I visited her, but I also saw the same condition of many other residents in the facility. I perceived that maybe in the recesses of their minds, they grieved over their helplessness. Each one had moved from the state of independence to the state of complete dependence.

Helpless states come to all of us—perhaps not permanently but certainly temporarily, in one form or another. Even strong people like Simon Peter, a disciple of Jesus, found himself in a helpless situation. On one occasion in Jesus's ministry, he walked on water from the shore of the sea to his disciples in a boat. Peter saw this phenomenon, and he too wanted to walk on the water. Jesus invited him to get out of the boat and walk to him. But after a few steps, Peter became frightened by the rough waves of the sea and began to sink. The situation turned into a helpless moment in his life: he was too far from the boat to get in it, and he was too far from the shore to swim the distance. He thought he was going to drown. Peter called out to Jesus, "Lord, save me!" It was the call from a helpless man.

On a hot summer day, I went to the doctor to get help for a sore throat. The doctor sensed that more was wrong than a simple sore throat. He sent me to another doctor to get an aspiration, which involves the penetration of a needle into the throat to get a biopsy. Several days later I returned to my throat doctor for the results. He diagnosed me with cancer. He told me I would have to have six doses of chemotherapy and thirty-five radiation treatments. He also said I would have to have a feeding tube for three or four months. After his diagnosis and schedule for treatment, I felt helpless. I did not have the strength or knowledge of how to help myself. I became totally dependent on medicine, radiation, and medical personnel.

This experience with cancer brought a sense of powerlessness in my life. I did not have the strength to teach my classes. I did not have the attention span to read or to watch television. Reading, writing, teaching, and traveling had to be put on hold. I became confined to a chair and to the monotonous passing of time. My feelings of worth and value were threatened. Eric Cassell, a doctor at Cornell University, wrote, "If I had to pick the aspect of illness that is most destructive to the sick, I would choose the loss of control."[5] Some situations like this last a lifetime, while others come and go. Whatever the time span of suffering, a sense of helplessness will appear. It is a prominent symptom of suffering and pain.

A fourth symptom of pain is the distance that suffering brings. A barrier goes up between us and even our closest friends. The sufferer suddenly senses a new isolation between them and almost everyone who has not experienced what they are going through. People you once felt close to may seem to drift away, and others may avoid you in your time of affliction. The resulting loneliness is perpetuated by a lack of meaningful contact and dialogue. Your friends have been struck with incompetency—they do not know what to say or do. Perhaps they fear that they may be drawn into the sufferer's pain themselves. During my moments of pain, I also found myself not even wanting people to visit me.

Indeed, a great gulf existed between Job and his friends. The four men differed in their feelings about each other. Job's friends acted with a judgmental spirit toward him. They made him feel guilty, and they were always telling Job the reason for his problem. These friends felt that Job had caused his own pain. Job and his friends also experienced differences in their theology. The friends ventilated the current theology of the day that suffering was caused by sin, and the more one sinned the more one suffered. Job admitted his sinfulness, but he did not know the reason he suffered. To him, his suffering was a great mystery. Neither Job nor his friends realized that suffering could come upon anyone, anytime, for unexplainable reasons.

Sometimes severe suffering changes people. Timothy Keller wrote, "Severe suffering turns you into a different person and some of the people you once felt affinity for no longer look the same to you."[6] What causes this distance, aloofness, or isolation that suffering brings? It could be as simple as the fact that some people have a tendency to avoid hurting people. Keeping our distance from someone in pain seems to be the most comfortable approach. Bad situations cause some people to feel uneasy. Distance can also be caused by empathetic imagination. When an observer is near a sick person, the observer may begin to feel they have the same illness. Heart attack victims tell their friends about the warning of chest pains before the attack, and their friends begin to feel that they have chest pains, too. Cancer patients tell loved ones the symptoms they had, and their loved ones begin to feel that they have the same symptoms.

Distance can also be caused by feelings of incompetence. People will associate with their hurting friend, but they do not know what to say or do when they are with them. They lack the knowledge of what they could do to help. They also feel awkward when they don't know what to say. Of course, Job's friends—Eliphaz, Bildad, and Zophar—had the opposite reaction. They thought they knew exactly what caused Job's suffering and what he could do to cure it. Their knowledge came from skewed traditional theology and an inadequate remedy of calling Job to repent. The friends thought Job suffered because of his sin and that the level of his suffering was equal to the greatness of his sin. The more Job and his friends talked, the greater the distance grew between them.

Testimonies from people in pain have confirmed the growing distance between them and their friends. They noticed their friends' avoidance.

People who once regularly contacted them rarely visited or called. The sufferers say, "I wonder what happened to _____. I never see or hear from him anymore. I miss the text messages and the emails from my friend." People in pain also say, "Conversations with _____ seem strained. She acts uncomfortable when she visits me. She seems as if she wants to get away." This distance brings loneliness to the sufferer, and that means the absence of a former meaningful relationship.

The fifth noticeable symptom of pain is the presence of negative emotions. Within the human temperament, various complex emotions exist. These help us express positive or negative reactions to external stimuli. Good emotions include ecstasy, elation, happiness, jubilation, gaiety, and many other pleasant feelings. Bad emotions include anxiety, distress, dread, uneasiness, and numerous other negative feelings. Suffering produces negative emotions, one of which is low self-esteem. In most cases, distressing circumstances contribute greatly to low self-esteem. Broken relationships constitute one of the prominent causes of thinking badly about oneself. At these times, the situation affects one's thinking process. One can think they are not loved by their family, their friends, and even their God. Often, they allow themselves to believe the opinions that others have formed about them.

Damaged emotions work within our inner being to make us think that we are no longer competent. Losing a job makes us feel like a failure and fearful of the ability to get and to hold another job. Serious illnesses make us so weak that we cannot function in many life situations. Sufferers feel different than well people do. Divorce causes us to feel like a failure and to feel incompetent at being a good marriage partner. Every crisis in my life has affected my self-esteem, especially my broken marriage and my debilitating cancers. During my distressing time of going through a divorce, I knew that I had to seek help for my injured self-esteem. Someone recommended that I read David Seamands's book *Healing for Damaged Emotions*.[7] Seamands was a professor of pastoral ministry at Asbury Theological Seminary. His book helped me greatly—so much so that I sought to have a personal session with him. I made the appointment with him and drove a long distance. In my personal session, Seamands led me to see that "I am okay, but I am feeling too much that I am not okay." He pointed out that my excessive focus on "not okay" created low self-esteem. He said this focus was bringing feelings of inferiority, inadequacy, and self-condemnation. Seamands urged me to focus more on "I am okay." He told me that a healthy self-esteem comes from a balanced evaluation. On one hand, he told me to confess, "I am okay." On the other hand, he told me to confess, "I am not okay." Thinking too highly of myself was not a healthy self-image. Also, thinking too low of myself was certainly not a healthy self-image. He helped me more with the biblical story of the prodigal son. The son felt unworthy to be called a son because of his behavior. But the father welcomed him home as a son with numerous signs of sonship. So a healthy self-image involves the confession, "I am a sinner, but also I am a child of the Heavenly Father."

Numerous negative emotions may exist in one distressing situation. At some point anger may appear. Anger always exists in the human psyche, and painful situations lift the lid for it to appear in a negative manner. Anger can take many directions depending on the cause and context, and it can be taken out on objects or innocent bystanders. Anger can also take the direction of bitterness against people who have wronged you or let you down. If it is not controlled, anger can lead to resentment or hostility toward another person. Often, repressed anger toward others leads to coldness, aloofness, or silence. This silence has a tendency to feed the anger and cause it to grow. Though I dislike mentioning the fact, it is also true that it is possible to direct anger toward God. Sometimes it manifests after a traumatic event, like the death of a loved one. Maybe God understands a person's anger. The prophets and the psalmists expressed their anger toward God. Their life situations were so bad that they thought God was the legitimate target of their anger.

Two kindred emotions—fear and anxiety—show up early during distressing times. Severe turns along the path of life create a fear of what might be around the corner. Fear becomes prominent amid the other distresses of a person in pain. Giving in to fear makes the world around us an environment of discouragement and robs us of our perspective. It distorts our feelings about the future. The more fear grows within a person, the less a person is able to reason. And along with fear comes the emotion of anxiety. The word "anxious" comes from a Greek word meaning "to be divided or distracted." Hurtful situations cause us to be confused. Anxiety is a painful uneasiness of the mind that feeds on imagined, impending fears, choking our ability to discern life's essential meaning. We join anxiety with our doubts, expectations, and pressures, and it adds more to an already crowded life. It leads us to insert premature solutions. Thinking irrationally makes us even more anxious and afraid.

Something needs to be done during stressful times to acknowledge and to seek control of our fears and anxiety. Allowing these emotions to go unattended causes even greater distress. Let me share with you how I dealt with my own fears. First, I took the time to face them. I acknowledged that these fears were within me and that they were hindering my progress of dealing with my pain. Second, I confessed my fears to God and to competent counselors. They helped me see that I could be helped. Third, I came to the place where I realized that I needed someone outside of me to give me self-control. The fruit of the Spirit in Galatians 5:22 lists self-control as a product of the Holy Spirit. I asked for the Spirit's control, and gradually the Spirit helped me with my fears.

What did I do with my anxieties? A study of Jesus' teaching about worry recorded in Matthew 6:25–34 helped me greatly. Jesus' suggestions are quite simple but practical. First, he says that life is more than the things we worry about. Second, he notes that worry does no good. Third, he reminds us that God cares for us and will provide for what we need. Fourth, he urges his disciples to put God first. Fifth, and finally, Jesus encourages us to live one day at a time. These five suggestions of Jesus have been with me for decades as a prescription for my anxieties.

In addition to anger, fear, and anxiety, we all experience feelings of guilt. It especially torments people in pain. When we knowingly hurt another person or act against our values or convictions, we should experience guilt. It can help us to acknowledge that we have done wrong, and that is important. How we handle our guilty feelings helps us discern whether our spiritual and emotional development is healthy or unhealthy. Guilt can be a stimulant, a painful jolt to incite us to change. But sometimes we experience guilt for no rational reason. We are conscious of no deliberate wrong. A person will say, "I feel guilty and I cannot say why." Such unreasonable feelings of guilt can create endless unrest and torment. If we allow these irrational feelings to affect us, they can control our lives. They must be confronted with the intelligence God gave us.

The main question seems to be, "How can we combat our rational guilty feelings and accept them?" First, we need to recognize and acknowledge the reason we have guilty feelings. These feelings function to help us grow and mature even when our behavior has been hurtful to others.

Rational guilt needs to be confronted and confessed. It can challenge us to change our behavior. Second, when we do something wrong, we will have to accept that we cannot change the past. We must seek forgiveness, apologize, make amends when needed, and let it go. The more we focus our thinking on the idea that we need to do something else, the more it will continue to bother us. Third, we must recognize that perfection does not exist in anyone. Even our family or friends who appear to be perfect make mistakes. We should recognize human error and confess it.

Fourth, feelings of guilt should bring us to seek forgiveness from God, from others, and from ourselves. Forgiveness helps with our pain. The Scripture is clear that genuine repentance to God leads to forgiveness. Forgiveness means that the passionate God absorbs the hurt. Every human mistake hurts God, but God is willing to forgive all of them. Receiving God's forgiveness gives us the power and motivation to forgive others. Asking another person for forgiveness opens us to the possibility of a "yes" or "no" answer. The "yes" is a gift of grace. The "no" means that we have to tolerate with grace another person's unforgiving spirit. Because guilt hurts our inner self, it is important to forgive ourselves when God has forgiven us. Paul Tillich once said in a lecture, "The hardest thing for me to accept is the fact that God has accepted me even though I am unacceptable." Failing to forgive ourselves leads to torment rather than stimulating growth.

Resolving our guilt does not mean we are released from the consequences of our failures. We must live with these and make reparations for them. A painful reality is that sometimes we hurt another person very deeply, and even though we are sorry and the person forgives us, the consequence is that the relationship will never be the same again. Following Jesus' way of seeking forgiveness helps people who hurt. We gradually realize that Jesus uses guilt not as a means of torment but as a stimulant to growth and change. The torment is our doing.

Negative feelings of the person in pain contribute to depression. It is a feeling many people experience occasionally and some experience habitually. Times of distress cause most people to feel down or "in the dumps." Of course, not all depression comes from hurtful circumstances. Medical research now diagnoses certain states of depression as being physical in origin. A chemical imbalance results in depression that arises neither from life situations nor from the inability to cope with problems. Chemical imbalances can be treated with antidepressant medications. Of course, severe depression happens when a person has both a chemical imbalance and a distressing circumstance.

But the depression I am writing about here is the usual "down time" that comes from hurtful situations: loss of a loved one, a great disappointment, a failure, an illness, an accident, or a relational problem. At times, situational depression can be acute due to the seriousness of the situation, such as the sudden death of a friend or loved one or the diagnosis of cancer. Then there are "lows" we feel when we are hurt by another person's words or rejected for a job promotion.

Depression resulting from bad situations becomes a problem only when we neglect the depressing feelings. Then it persists and gets the best of us. Repression takes place when we try to hide painful and negative feelings within ourselves. Such repression leads to confused, distorted, and distressing thoughts and feelings. Sometimes situational depression requires medication and counseling for a period, but circumstantial depression can also be helped by self-expression. Sharing our feelings with someone we trust can help us sort things out. Depressed people need to talk; they need a friend who will listen and feel with them. Thank God I found many such friends! But talking with God may be the greatest source of help. I have had many "gut-level" conversations with God. The psalmist said, "Out of the depths I have cried to You, LORD. Lord, hear my voice!" (Psalm 130:1-2a). In our emptiness we can share our agony with God. We can allow God to touch, absorb, and heal our twisted thoughts.

What do we stuff away within ourselves? There are numerous repressed factors that contribute to depression. One of those factors is anxiety, which represents unreasonable fears about our lives. Many of our anxieties are illogical and unreasonable, yet they influence our lives and make them uncomfortable. Often, the answer to our repressed anxieties is openness with others about our hurts. A second contributing factor is repressed anger. Depression has been defined as "anger turned inward." Anger is often avoided and denied instead of recognized and expressed. People need to permit themselves to express their anger appropriately. When anger has been shared with another, a person gets the freedom to live a more comfortable and constructive life.

A third contributing factor to depression is negative thinking. Hurting people tend to be down on themselves. Worthless feelings multiply in their minds. People in pain become their own worst enemies through self-condemnation. Unreasonable, ridiculous conclusions need to be confronted. Negative feelings are often fueled by pressures of perfectionism. Unrealistic and irresponsible situations set us up for disappointment and further depression. But it is essential not to lose hope. It is easy to lose hope in others, in God, and in ourselves. Without hope, we succumb to feelings of helplessness. In episodes of depression, we need to search for the deeper meaning of what is happening to us. When we find meaning within our hurt, it can mobilize our lives in ways we never dreamed. Good things do come from bad situations in ways we may not always expect.

An analysis of human suffering can be a probing venture. It shows how infinitely complex and diverse a condition of affliction may be. The noticeable internal and external symptoms of self-absorption, psychosomatic feelings, helplessness, distance, and damaged emotions can be present to some degree in any hurtful situation. So the noticeable symptoms may exist proportionally in every person, but different personal responses assist people in dealing with their noticeable symptoms of pain in various ways.

### Notes

[1] Simone Weil, *Waiting for God* (New York: Routledge & Taylor Francis Group: 2009), 213–16.

[2] J. R. R. Tolkien, *The Lord of the Rings: The Two Towers* (Boston: Houghton Mifflin Press, 2004), 14.

[3] Weil, *Waiting for God*, 70.

[4] Max Lucado, *It's Not about Me* (Nashville: Integrity Publishers, 2004), 5.

[5] Quoted in Philip Yancey, *Where Is God When It Hurts?* 185.

[6] Timothy Keller, *Walking with God through Pain and Suffering* (New York: Penguin Books, 2013), 213.

[7] David Seamands, *Healing for Damaged Emotions* (Colorado Springs: David C. Cook, 1981).

## Chapter 5

# Confusing Voices

On my pilgrimage with the pains from a failed marriage and from several cancer treatments, I encountered many kinds of responses from people. Some people chose the route of avoidance. Relatives and friends knew about my distresses, but they kept their distance from me. Why? I do not think it was because they disliked me. I think that seeing me in pain from a marital breakup and in the pain of my cancers made them uncomfortable. Their absence reflected more about them than it did about me. Some probably felt that what happened in my marriage could happen in their own marriage—a thought they probably wanted to avoid. Some who heard of my different cancer diagnoses and physical pain may have imagined similar symptoms in their own lives, which may have caused them anxiety and fear. The most comfortable alternative for these people was to keep their distance and try not to think of my distresses.

Some people did choose to communicate with me or make a personal visit, but I noticed that these occasions were just a shade above avoidance. Though they did not avoid me, they were not "with me" when we conversed by phone or when they came to visit. Instead of listening attentively or engaging in meaningful dialogue with me, silence and guarded speech seemed to be their main activities. By their verbal and nonverbal communication, I could tell they were with me but did not empathize with me. My presence made them uncomfortable, and I could really detect their discomfort when I shared my feelings about my failed marriage or facts about my cancer detection and treatment. I could actually detect their relief when our phone conversations drew to a close and our personal visits came to an end. For some, seeing my deteriorated physical condition gave them a hypochondriacal experience. They perceived that they were experiencing the same physical symptoms I had.

While many avoided me in my pain, others reached out to with me with care. I treasured those who had the courage to call or visit. I profited greatly from many people who sent me cards with handwritten messages of encouragement. Letters, texts, and emails came to me from caring people. The care of Jane, my wife, made my pilgrimage more bearable. My doctors, nurses, and other medical personnel responded to me with genuine kindness. Some relatives, many friends, and even people I did not know reached out to me with encouragement.

But one thing surprised me when some people communicated with me. They gave confusing messages—messages that brought greater hurt to me instead of comfort and understanding. These people practiced their theology with me by telling me why my suffering happened. Others engaged in "homemade counseling," telling me what I should and should not do. These people practiced the art of omniscience and harsh human judgments. A few diagnosed the precise reason for my divorce. Several suggested medicines I needed to take and doctors I needed to see for my cancers.

In the deepest part of me, I felt that people did not know what to say when they heard about my pain and observed my symptoms of hurt. But some felt that they needed to say something. Some visitors and communicators had a hard time sitting in silence and listening to my feelings of distress. In their minds, they felt that their contact with me was worthless unless they spoke words. I guess because I was a minister, most people thought they had to bring God into the conversation. In most cases my contacts had a healthy biblical perspective of God and suffering. But unfortunately, many confusing voices reflected cultural concepts of God, humanistic pictures of God, and biblical inaccuracies about God. I had hoped that my Christian friends would bring comfort to what I was going through. Instead, I heard voices from people that led to confusion, not consolation. A few religious people were the most depressing, irritating part of my journey with pain. I felt that a faith based on the Great Physician should bring peace, not confusion, at a time of intense distress. I will share in greater detail some of the voices that confused me. Perhaps this will help readers be ready for the voices that come when they go through pain.

The first and foremost confusing voice came from traditional theologians. To consider their idea, we need to return to the story of Job. The news of Job's unparalleled series of catastrophes spread rapidly across the

Eastern lands, and soon three friends journeyed to bring Job comfort. Over in Teran, a city of Edom famous for its philosophies, lived a sage named Eliphaz, a friend of Job. In the tribe of Shual, probably a roaming tribe in the Eastern land, lived another friend named Bildad, noted for his wisdom. In the city of Naamah, "now of uncertain location," lived Job's philosopher friend, Zophar. When the news of the troubles of Job reached these friends, they made an appointment to visit Job and comfort him.[1]

When the three friends arrived at Job's residence, they did not know him. His physical condition and appearance had been altered by his calamities. When they saw Job, the friends were overcome with grief. They were so shocked at his pitiful state that they expressed their grief in dramatic fashion—they wept aloud, tore their robes, and sprinkled dust on their heads. Then, for a symbolic seven days and nights, they sat on the ground by Job in silence, a gesture of compassion.

The silence of the friends undoubtedly consoled Job. But after seven days, Job heard the confusing voices of Eliphaz, Bildad, and Zophar. The writer of the book of Job recorded for thirty chapters the dialogue between Job and his friends. After Job's opening speech, there were three cycles of speeches, in which each friend spoke in turn and Job answered. Job and his friends discussed the problem of why Job, an apparently innocent and righteous man, experienced such unparalleled suffering and loss. The dialogue soon ranges over God's dealing with people and includes the meaning of life and the character of God.

All of Job's friends advanced the same theological argument. Their theology involved the orthodox explanation of suffering in those days, known by biblical scholars as "Deuteronomic theology." Suffering was God's punishment for sin. They reasoned that if a person did good, peace and prosperity would follow. The friends' philosophy was based on human beings' knowledge of God. Since God is just and holy, it is unthinkable that evil should prosper or good suffer loss. They felt that the Judge of the earth must do right. Any earthly judge would reward the good and punish the evil; God, they surmised, cannot do less. The friends' argument can be summarized in a neat syllogism—Major premise: Since God is just, God always punishes sin with suffering. Minor premise: Job is undergoing exceptionally great suffering. Inescapable conclusion: Job is an exceptionally great sinner. Job's friends recommended that he admit that he had sinned, that all his piety had been a mockery, and that his noble life had been a sham.

Job answered his friends by advocating his righteousness. Though he admitted he was not perfect before God, he insisted that his punishment was far more than his sins and failures deserved. Job admitted that God punishes sin with suffering. However, he found two problems with his friends' theology. One was the practical problem—it did not work out that simply in everyday life. He said that he had seen men steal the widow's ox and the orphan's inheritance and still get by, living to an old age in peace and prosperity (cf. Job 21:7–9, 13–16). Then Job saw the problem of people being good for selfish reasons. If by keeping the Ten Commandments people can be assured of "health, happiness, and prosperity," Job claimed, they will be righteous for what they can get out of it for themselves.

Though Job proclaimed his innocence, he was at a loss to answer why all of his troubles had befallen him. Job's statements ranged from bitter questions of God's goodness to great expressions of faith and trust, from fierce rebellions and bleak despair of his lot in life to some of the most profound insights into the ways of God. Goaded by his friends' increasingly bitter and unfair accusations, Job tenaciously clung to his own righteousness.

I must admit that I admire the beauty of expression and rhetoric of these three theologians. I also admit that there is much truth in what they said. They emphasized the glory, wisdom, and justice of God with profound figures of speech. They painted with broad strokes the sins of the human race. They pointed out Job's pride and self-righteousness. But, in my opinion, the great fallacy of the friends' argument is that they left no room for God's grace and mercy. Their great failure is that they failed to meet Job's needs. William B. Ward gave a good description of how these friends failed Job. When he needed sympathy, they offered argument; when he needed understanding, they offered dogmatics; when he longed for the fellowship of friends, they offered condemnation for him and self-righteousness for themselves. They tried to answer human need with cold logic.[2]

The theology of Job's friends did not just exist in the Eastern lands thousands of years ago. One can see the theology of sin bringing punishment from God throughout Hebrew history. We also read of Deuteronomic theology encountered by Jesus and his disciples. There was an occasion mentioned in John 9 of Jesus walking with his disciples. They saw a man born blind from birth. The disciples were puzzled. Their Deuteronomic theology did not fit the occasion. They asked Jesus, "Who sinned, this man or his parents?" Jesus answered them not with philosophical Deuteronomic reasoning but with compassion to help the blind man. He solved the man's problem by healing him, not by diagnosing the reason that he suffered.

People still tell suffering people that suffering is God's punishment for sin. People in pain ask, "What have I done, that this suffering should happen to me?" When I served as a pastor, I heard the confusing voice of Deuteronomic theology, the same idea espoused by Job's friends. Three visitors had come to visit one of the senior adults of our church. This senior adult suffered greatly from numerous ailments. I came to make a pastoral call to the lady, and I joined the other three ladies who were with her. My presence seemed to turn the conversation to these ladies' thoughts of God and the reasons for suffering. The lady who suffered from a heart condition, lung disease, and crippling arthritis interrupted our conversation by asking, "Pastor, what has caused my suffering?" I was stunned into silence. Before I could speak a word, the other visitors answered the lady's question. They said, "Maude, you ought to know the answer to your question. You know how the four of us lived a rough life during our high school days. Now God is punishing you for your sins." Wow! I froze because I could not believe what I heard. I thought I was in the land of Uz with Job and his friends. I wondered why the ladies admitted their past rough life but only applied God's punishment to Maude. I heard the confusing voice of rationalistic theology that was void of the biblical revelation about suffering and void of compassion toward Maude.

Is the voice of Job's friends the only choice about God, sin, and suffering? No, there is the voice of biblical revelation. The Bible has narratives that can enrich our understanding of God and suffering. These stories greatly affected my attitudes, giving me a new frame of mind for facing adversity. The narratives begin with the doctrines of creation and the Fall. Genesis 1 and 2 relate the story about human beings put into a world without death and suffering. The troubles we see today were evidently not part of God's original design for the world and human beings.

The biblical narrative continues in Genesis 3 and relates the origin of the world's darkness. It appeared and unfolded out of human refusal to allow God to be the Lord of their lives. When humans turned from God, their relationship with God was broken. It was the beginning of the Fall. This human brokenness with God led to brokenness within one's self and with other human beings. It also meant brokenness within human nature. The Fall meant that the original design of the world was broken. This Fall resulted in suffering and death. The doctrine of the Fall gives a helpful understanding of the origin of suffering.

The universal Fall rejects the idea that people who suffer more are always worse than people who suffer less. Timothy Keller responds to the bad theology of Job's friends by saying, "The world is too fallen and deeply broken to divide into a neat pattern of good people having good lives and bad people having bad lives. The brokenness of the world is inherited by the entire human race. The individual sufferer is not necessarily receiving a due payment for specific wrongdoings."[3] We must never say that every particular occasion of suffering is caused by a particular sin. But to be true to biblical theology, we need to say that suffering and death in general is a natural consequence of God's just judgment upon our sin.[4]

The story of sin and suffering concludes in Revelation 21 and 22 with a picture of a redeemed heaven and earth. Everything lost in the Fall will be restored in the final redemption. This redemption involves the abolition of evil, pain, suffering, and death brought by God's power to resurrect believers' physical bodies and give "a new heaven and a new earth." Human beings and creation will be transformed into what God intended them to be. J. R. R. Tolkien envisioned the end of history as a time when "everything sad is going to come untrue."[5]

Job's friends emphasized sin and suffering, but they pointed out that Job's suffering was due to specific sins instead of adjusting their theology to human suffering as a general consequence of sin. While the voice of traditional theology confused me, the narrative of biblical theology corrected me. Confusion comes to sufferers not only from traditional theologians but also from the voice of enthusiastic cheerleaders—people who use cliché statements to try to lift the depressed spirits of people in pain. Well-intentioned visitors try to move conversations to a purely positive note, attempting to shift the conversation to happy thoughts in an unhappy time.

Some cheerleaders share Scripture verses in attempts to evoke hopeful thoughts. Several cheerleaders contacted me after my wife's departure.

Some of them said to me, "God has revealed to me that your wife is going to return." Those words gave me temporary comfort. For years they continued periodically with that promising word. As time passed, it seemed that my wife was not going to return. After a three-and-a-half-year absence, she filed for divorce and married someone else shortly thereafter. My enthusiastic visitors kept contacting me, but they said nothing about their "cheers" regarding my wife's return. Cheerleaders mean well, but their messages are not always true. Maybe the visitors could have talked about God's intentional will for all married couples to remain married. But God's will is not always obeyed—people can choose to disobey it. God gives that permission. My wife had the freedom to follow her will. God gives people that kind of permission so they can be free and not controlled by others.

Other cheerleaders came to me in my cancer experiences, and they said, "You look great!" I loved their complimentary words, but I knew the real appearance of my countenance. I observed my physical condition manifested by the loss of more than twenty pounds, the paleness of my skin, and my lack of energy. I knew the intention of the cheerleaders—they wanted to lift my spirits. I remember one person who, in every card she sent, advised me to work on having a good attitude. This person's "cheer" came in times of chemo and radiation. During days and nights of nausea and tiredness, it was extremely difficult for me to obey my enthusiastic writer.

Of course, many people who visited me during my sicknesses and my marital breakup were religious. They quoted Bible verses to me. But with my formal biblical training, I recognized that not all of their quotes captured what the verses truly meant. One helpful Bible professor I had in seminary gave me a great line about interpreting the Bible. He said, "A Bible passage cannot mean what it never meant. It cannot say to us what it did not say to the original readers." I have held tenaciously to the professor's statement in interpreting the Bible. One example of a religious person who quoted such Scripture to me focused on 1 Thessalonians 5:18—"in everything give thanks." That person said, "You need to come to the place in your suffering where you can thank God for your pain. Suffering is God's will, and God knows what is best for you." Frankly, I had a hard time thanking God for my wife leaving me. Also, I do not remember a day when I thanked God for giving me an alcoholic father. At no time during my diagnoses and treatments of five cancers did I ever say, "Thank you, God, for my cancer."

My visitor's quote of "in everything give thanks" motivated me to try to understand what the writer of 1 Thessalonians meant by that statement. The author of Thessalonians was writing to people who had recently accepted Christ. In this first letter to the Thessalonians, the writer gave important doctrines of the Christian faith. He closed the letter with twelve commands on how to apply these doctrines (cf. 1 Thessalonians 5:12–22). In one section of these commands, the writer gave the following series: "Rejoice always; pray without ceasing; in everything give thanks; for this is God's will for you in Christ Jesus" (5:16–18). In the first command, "rejoice always," the writer implied that rejoicing does not depend on life situations. Rejoicing in the context of 1 Thessalonians 5:16a is an attitude generated by a relationship to Christ.[6]

The admonition "in everything give thanks" resembles the meaning of "rejoice always." It does not mean that the believer will be in a giddy state of thanksgiving all the time. Our days can bring sorrow; people can disappoint us; storms may happen. Nevertheless, the believer is to be thankful *not* for the life situation that brings sorrow but for the presence and strength of God in that situation. Paul Tillich wrote about gratitude, "It is a mood of joy, but more than a mood, more than a transitory emotion. It is a state of being."[7] So the encourager got it wrong. I was not to thank God for the cancer or the divorce. I was to thank God for being with me and helping me in all circumstances. I learned that gratitude did not come from reaction to situations but from a relationship with God.

One visitor choosing to console me said, "Harold, God intended all of your suffering. God wanted to teach you something. You know the Bible says, 'All things work together for the good.'" It was a confusing voice rather than a comforting one. The remark from the visitor came from Romans 8:28. As with my previous techniques, I chose to study what Romans 8:28 meant to the original readers. I first looked at the subject of the sentence. It did not indicate that "all things" work together for good. Instead, it indicated that "God causes all things to work together for good to those who love God, to those who are called according to His purpose" (Romans 8:28). Romans 8:28 does not mean that everything that happens is good. It is not. There is unmitigated evil in the world. Furthermore, this verse does not mean that everything is going to work out good for all people. The promise of the good is only "for those who love God" and who are "called according to His purpose." God can do great works out of suffering for those who walk with God.

Most people define" good" in terms of health, wealth, and success. The good promised in the Roman passage defines good as a growing conformity to Christlikeness. Romans 8:28 needs to be read along with Romans 8:29. In Bible study, this is called putting a verse in its context, which means to examine what comes before the verse and what comes after the verse. Verse 29 says, "For those whom He foreknew, He also predestined to become conformed to the image of His Son, so that He would be the firstborn among many brothers and sisters." To accomplish God's purpose, God can use all things—the good as well as the bad—and mix them together for our spiritual good. No experience has to be wasted if we commit it to God. God's divine providence can embrace it all—failure as well as success, illness as well as health. Sometimes illness, hardships, rejection, and failure can be the means God uses to shape our lives into God's image.

I did not always understand what God was doing during my marital breakup and illnesses. I certainly did not welcome the hardships. But as my walk with God continued, I came to see that God wanted to form my character, not just give me comfort. I did know that the distresses in my life were bad, but God wanted to use these problems to make me a more Christlike person. My cheerleader friend needed to change his words from "all things work together" to "God works all things together."

In addition to the voices of traditional theologians and enthusiastic cheerleaders, I had some people to say to me, "You need to seek the counsel of a faith healer." A few people wanted to lead me in a healing process. They began by telling me that suffering was not God's will. They told me to have faith and that, if I had enough faith, God would heal me of my cancer. These voices of faith healing referred to an incident in Jesus' ministry when his disciples could not heal a man's son. They asked Jesus why it did not happen. Jesus answered by telling them it was because of the littleness of their faith (cf. Matthew 17:19–20). These religious leaders told me to simply name my problem and in faith claim the victory. The idea of mustering up faith seems awfully exhausting, and I could never decide what it meant. I do believe in divine healing, but I have problems with faith healers who offer a formula that always works.

Another popular verse quoted by faith healers appears in Matthew 21:22: "And whatever you ask in prayer, believing, you will receive it all." Many make these words of Jesus a successful formula for human healing: name your problem, claim God's answer, and celebrate the victory of healing. In some cases, when people use the formula and healing does not happen, the faith healer says, "You just did not have enough faith."

What did Jesus mean about asking, believing, and receiving in Matthew 21:22? To understand what Jesus meant, one must examine the context in which the words were originally spoken. The text fits in the context of Matthew 12:18–22, where Jesus gave lessons about a barren fig tree. Jesus taught that one did not have to be fruitless. There is a divine resource that leads to fruitfulness. In the New Testament, fruit means the character reflected in Jesus' life. Fruit bearing happens to believers who "abide in Christ" and "ask." Jesus used the term "believing" in Matthew 21:22 to refer to an inward relationship with God. It also refers to a continuing relationship with God—"abiding." If a person opens their life to Christ, fruit comes. So, in Matthew 21:22, Jesus seems to be talking about fruit bearing more than faith healing.

Each episode I had with cancer caused me to want healing. As the cancer diagnoses progressed, I wondered more than ever about healing. I studied the Scripture. I read Kate Bowler's books *Blessed: A History of the American Prosperity Gospel* and *Everything Happens for a Reason and Other Lies I've Loved*. In the first book she academically researches the believers who practice the "prosperity gospel." Bowler writes, "This book seeks to share how millions of Americans come to see money, health, and good fortune as divine."[8] In her second book, she reports how, at thirty-five, everything in her life seemed to point toward blessing. Then she was diagnosed with Stage 4 colon cancer. Bowler says she began to think about getting from one good action to another rather than being cured or dying.[9]

After praying, studying the Scripture, and listening to many people, I came to some conclusions about faith healing. First, I resolved that the Scripture speaks of divine healing rather than faith healing. The healing depends on the sovereignty of God rather that the efforts of humans to have the right amount of faith. Second, I admitted that I believed in the healing ministry of Jesus. The Gospel writers portray Jesus as one who had authority over sickness, nature, handicap, the demonic world, and even death. I resolved that Jesus still has the power to perform miracles whenever and with whomever he wishes today.

Third, as I read the Gospel accounts of Jesus' ministry, I noticed that he did not heal every person he saw. Does that mean he played favorites? Of course not. Jesus loved every person, sick and well. Then why did he not heal everyone? The answer to that question came with the issue of the kingdom of God. The kingdom means "the rule of God." When Jesus came to earth, he healed to demonstrate the arrival of the kingdom. But the kingdom was not fully expressed in Jesus' earthly ministry. If he had healed everyone, the kingdom would have arrived fully. The kingdom will fully come when Jesus returns. All evil, suffering, and death will be eliminated. Believers pray "Thy kingdom come" in anticipation of the full reign of Christ. Meanwhile, on earth believers need to engage in the kingdom agenda with the realization that the full reign of God is "not yet."

Fourth, I realized that not all miracles performed on earth have permanent results. Lazarus died and Jesus raised him back to life, but Lazarus also died again later. People healed from illnesses recovered for a while, and they became ill again. I remember an experience with a person who was gravely ill with leukemia. He stayed in a bubble at M. D. Anderson Hospital in Houston, Texas, for eighty-five days. I went to see him on the eighty-third day at the request of his family. He was threatening to get out of the bubble. On the morning of his eighty-fifth day, I sat outside waiting to talk with him on an intercom. That morning his doctor appeared and told me, "Preacher, I want to give you the honor of unzipping the bubble." I did, and the doctor and the patient's wife went inside. I waited until they left, and then I visited the patient. Conversation came slowly. Finally, I said, "Bill, God has done a miracle with you." Bill responded with a statement that taught me a lot about miracles: "Yes, pastor, God healed me, but remember no miracle is permanent."

Fifth, I became convinced that God worked miracles all throughout my cancer experiences. At this writing, recent scans indicate that no cancer exists in my body NOW, but I realize the healing could last only for a short time. My ultimate healing of all pain and suffering will be when Jesus returns and I get a new body and live in a regenerated heaven and earth.

Words have great power to communicate. By means of words, inner attitudes are shared with others. The spoken word has power either to help or to hurt a person in pain. Hearing theologians tell us that if we are good we will receive good things, but if we are bad we will receive bad things has the power to increase guilt and produce shame. It makes us ask questions like "What particular sin or sins caused my suffering?" and "Why do so many bad people not suffer and so many good people suffer?" and "How could a good God, a just God, a loving God allow so much painful misery and anguish?" Words from theologians often take a logical, philosophical approach, but people in pain need sympathy and compassion more than mental gymnastics. The pain caused by the words of people's responses can exceed the pain of the suffering itself. Upon hearing several people lecture to me about "Deuteronomic theology," I exclaimed with Job, "I have heard many things like these; Miserable comforters are you all!" (Job 16:2). When cheerleaders exploited my emotions, telling me to "cheer up—everything is going to be fine," their words hurt me more than helped me. Maybe comfort did come for a moment with their cheers. But the cheer and goodwill wishes left as I faced another day of pain.

Followers of faith healing confused me with their formula: "Name your suffering; claim healing with your faith; and celebrate the victory." I got through the first two maxims, but I experienced failure with celebrating victory. It did not come. I did not question God's healing power, but I did feel that my faith was not good enough. Many who have asked for healing and not received it ask, "How much faith is enough?" After deep contemplation, I realized that I believed in divine healing more than faith healing. Whom God heals depends on God's sovereign choice.

People did speak confusing words to me during my pilgrimage of pain. I have shared how they hurt me. But thankfully, more people spoke comforting words than confusing ones, and I am deeply grateful for those people. Many comforted me with short visits, brief telephone calls, and succinct text messages, and I came to realize that authentic comforters represented God's agent. I could feel that my comforters loved me as Jesus loved me. They resolved to stay connected with me. They communicated care. Their words seemed to come from a heart of compassion. They refrained from being legalistic or judgmental. Instead, they gave me a picture of grace. Many times, conversations with these people felt like a visit from the Great Physician.

Many became fellow sufferers with me. By that, I mean divorced people talked to me about forgiving any fault in my partner and in myself. They told me that I would get through the dark times and learn from my heartache. They accepted me as a flawed person in need of grace. Their words helped with my anxiety, shame, guilt, and disappointment over a failed marriage. People with the same kind of cancer told me of their treatments. They encouraged me to depend on God's strength and face each day as a gift. Fellow sufferers became "wounded healers" to each other. No written words could communicate the depth of comfort, encouragement, strength, and counsel I received from people who had gone through a divorce and from people who had gone through cancer.

The words of others taught me to be careful with my own words. I prayed that the words of my mouth and the meditations of my heart would communicate courage and comfort to others.

## Notes

[1] William B. Ward, *Out of the Whirlwind: A Study of the Book of Job* (Richmond, VA: John Knox Press, 1962), 37.

[2] Ibid., 43.

[3] Timothy Keller, *Walking with God through Pain and Suffering* (New York: Penguin Books, 2013), 114–15.

[4] Ibid., 115.

[5] Quoted in Philip Keller, *Walking with God through Pain and Suffering*, 118.

[6] Linda McKinnish Bridges, "1 & 2 Thessalonians," in *Smyth & Helwys Bible Commentary*, edited by R. Alan Culpepper (Macon, GA: Smyth & Helwys, 2008), 162–63.

[7] Paul Tillich, *The Eternal Now* (New York: Charles Scribner's, 1963), 176–77.

[8] Kate Bowler, *Blessed: A History of the Prosperity Gospel* (New York: Oxford University Press, 2013), 7.

[9] Kate Bowler, *Everything Happens for a Reason and Other Lies I've Loved* (New York: Random House, 2018), 8.

# Chapter 6

# Searching for Help

In the city where I live, there is a plumbing, heating, and air conditioner business that has an unusual name. It is called "Hep." The company has a unique television advertisement. It shows a dramatic scene of a husband and wife distressed over a broken pipe at the kitchen sink. Water shoots several feet into the air, flooding the kitchen. The wife exclaims, "We need help!" The husband appears to be troubled and asks, "But where do we find good help?" Of course, viewers of the commercial answer the question: "You can get good help with 'Hep.'"

That advertisement became a comparison with the conversation people in pain have, especially for me. When I hurt, I often said both inwardly and outwardly, "I need help!" Along with the exclamation often came the question, "But where can I find good help?" The help I needed had to be good for me to manage, cope, reduce, or eliminate my hurt. In my conversations, readings, and observations, numerous suggestions came to me about how I could be helped. These are some of the recommendations I received: Secure a compassionate, competent counselor; practice yoga; go to a pain clinic; exercise regularly and eat healthy. No one recommended alcohol or drugs to me, but many people seek them for help. I tried some of the suggestions, but I did not find the help I wanted or needed.

In my inward dialogue with the television advertisement, I still said, "I need help!" But my question in the dialogue changed to, "But where can I get the best help?" My background with the Bible, the inward support of the Holy Spirit, and the Christian community took me toward practical exercises that appeared to be higher and deeper than all of the previous helpful suggestions. My Christian experience furnished me with the resources to help with my pain. I selected four active disciplines that have given me my best help: praying, uniting, lamenting, and enduring.

Praying was my best daily help. Taking the time to pray and learning the pattern of praying has required a lifetime of learning, not just a time during my pilgrimage with pain. Years ago I read Andrew Murray's book *With Christ in the School of Prayer*.[1] He likened the practice of prayer to a lifetime of union with Christ where one gradually learns to communicate with God. My first time of praying came early in my life. My parents taught me to pray a simple prayer before meals: "God is great; God is good; Let us thank him for our food. Amen." They taught me a prayer to say at bedtime: "Now I lay me down to sleep. I pray the Lord my soul to keep. If I should die before I wake, I pray the Lord my soul to take. Amen." These simple prayers taught me to acknowledge God, thank God for his gifts, and ask for God's protection. The repetitive engagement with these simple prayers represented a kindergarten experience, but I learned the importance of prayer in my life.

According to Andrew Murray, I enlisted in the school of prayer when I became a believer. My union with Christ motivated me to mature in my conversations with God. Unfortunately, I remember childish and selfish concerns in my early prayers. I asked God many times for it not to rain because my dad and I planned to go fishing. I asked God to help me pass algebra tests. I also prayed to God that my school would win football games. Fortunately, God did not flunk me in the school of prayer. God had grace and allowed me to learn about prayer and to mature in the process. Learning to pray was a struggle. Discarding my desires and developing a passion for God's will challenged me. My journey in the school of prayer has been a long one. I have not graduated yet. I am still learning how to pray. However, I am profiting from the joys of the journey with Christ in the discipline of prayer.

Tough times drove me to serious prayer. I really wanted help. Let me share a learning experience among the many I have had in prayer. In my marital separation, I prayed fervently for God to bring back my wife so we could restore our family. Many of my friends prayed for her return, and they sought to reason with her to return. As months and years passed with her still away from me, I became weary, frustrated, and angry. Anger began to creep into my prayers. One night in my praying I became angry with God. I prayed, "Why, God, did you allow this to happen to me? I have preached your word, cared for the sick and dying, and I did my best to be a good husband. Why don't you bring her home? I am mad!" After my ranting episode with God, I became silent. Actually, I became afraid that God was going to strike me dead for speaking so harshly.

What did I learn about that prayer? I learned that God will allow us to be honest in prayer. Later, I realized how little I understood God's love and goodness. One new question did come from my silence. What if my wife did not want to return? I learned that prayer is not a manipulation of another person. God respects our will and allows us to do what we want to do. I then prayed that God would put people and circumstances in my wife's life that might cause her to change her mind. I attributed her failure to return to God's mystifying respect for human freedom and the refusal to coerce.

The lessons on prayer continued in another dimension. Later, God had lessons for me as I faced cancer. In 2001, I was diagnosed with prostate cancer. In 2015, I was diagnosed with thyroid cancer, and in 2016, I was told that I had throat cancer. In 2016, the cancer spread from my throat to my left lung, and then in 2018, it spread to my right lung. Each time I had a body scan and a biopsy, I prayed fervently that the diagnosis would be negative. But each biopsy came back positive for cancer and required diligent treatment. The cancer experiences revealed that I had made progress in the school of prayer. Instead of expecting God to take care of every negative thing that happened to me, I came to the place where I accepted that bad things will happen to me in my life. When bad situations arise, we have to pray for strength, stamina, and the attitude that God will help us. During long hours in the infusion room and amid the painful side effects, I could sense the presence and power of God to help me cope.

During my cancer treatment, I also learned the valuable art of thanksgiving. I thanked God for Jane, a real companion and fabulous caregiver. I thanked God for leading me to excellent cancer specialists at the University Hospital. I thanked God for a community of friends who contacted me, encouraged me, and prayed for me. In 2019, I thanked God that my body scans revealed the presence of no new cancer. Cancer could return to me, or it could come to anyone. But we can thank God in advance that God cares for us and will help us. Nothing helped my prayer life better than the Lord's Prayer. This prayer has also been called the model prayer because it furnishes us with practical instruction on how to pray according to God's way. The prayer begins with an invocation—"Our Father, who is in heaven, Hallowed be Your name" (Matthew 6:9). The first words of the prayer remind us to recall who God is. Only then can we come to our loving Father in heaven with appropriate humility and reverence.

When we orient ourselves toward God and remember who God is, the content of our prayers will be radically affected. First, God's concerns will be given priority ("Your kingdom come. Your will be done, On earth as it is in heaven" [6:10]). After putting heavenly things first, we can then express our earthly needs to our heavenly Father. In this second half of the prayer, the possessive adjective changes from "Your" to "us" as we turn from God's agenda to our needs ("Give us this day our daily bread," "forgive us our debts," "deliver us from evil" [6:11-13]).

The last words, which follow in the King James Version, were not a part of the original prayer and are not contained in modern translations. The New American Standard Bible translation includes the words in a bracket. Scholars feel that these words were added by a sound instinct of the early church. They give us the reason that it is proper for us to offer the prayer: "For thine is the kingdom, and the power, and the glory, for ever. Amen" (6:13b, KJV). It serves to end the prayer as it began in the thought of the sovereignty and glory of God. In looking over this prayer numerous times, I found that Jesus first put forth the interests of God, following those with human needs. I had to be careful not to reverse the order of the model prayer by praying for material blessings more earnestly than I did for spiritual blessings—for God's glory, God's rule, and God's will.

This prayer became a model for my praying. I repeated it frequently. Often, I pray using every part of it to offer my prayer to God. Many times I have recited the Lord's Prayer during extremely difficult times. The prayer brings me comfort and offers me direction for my prayer agenda. It helps me with my needs, not my wants. I would strongly suggest for anyone in great hurt to turn to the model prayer to help them be more effective in praying.

Now let me share another action involved in my pilgrimage as a Christian. My seminary education prepared me professionally and personally for my life as a Christian. Both the professors and the courses helped me practically in my Christian life. One of my New Testament professors, whose name was Dr. Ray Frank Robbins, helped me learn to read the Greek New Testament. He had the unique ability to help students understand the meanings of Greek words and how they were used in New

Testament times. Robbins had the special gift of explaining the meanings of Greek words and applying them to life today.

I remember a lecture Robbins gave on the meaning of faith in the New Testament. His lecture began with the Greek word for faith (*pistis*), a noun. Robbins spoke of another Greek word—*pisteuo*—used as a verb and translated as "believe." The professor created a beautiful picture with the root stem of these two Greek words. You can see the similarity of the two words even if you cannot read Greek. Robbins told the class that the root of these Greek words was *peith*. The New Testament writers used "believe" and "faith" to refer to the act of bringing together, connecting, or joining. Of course, the biblical writers used the words to refer to God joining God's life with a human being. Robbins further taught that believing was not a head knowledge or a creedal confession; indeed, he coined the word "faithing" to describe a person's faith or trust in the Lord. To believe or to "faith" meant that God's life, which is called eternal life, joins with human life in a personal relationship.

Other words in the New Testament were used synonymously with "uniting." Jesus' teaching on the vine and the branches recorded in John 15 paints a corresponding picture: a branch had life because of its joining to the vine. Jesus used the word "abide" to describe this union. The apostle Paul used a similar phrase to describe his relationship with Christ—the expression "in Christ." Paul used the phrase or its derivative 164 times in his letters. The apostle John used the word "abiding" more than twenty times in 1 John. Indeed, the predominant metaphor of 1 John is "abide." John spoke of God's nature as life, righteousness, and love. To be joined with Christ meant that a person shared God's nature—that is, the believer walked in the light, obeyed Christ's commands out of inward righteousness, and loved in the same way Christ loved. These three illustrated to me how being a Christian meant being connected with and abiding in Christ.

The term "uniting" became my favorite word to describe my Christian life. It became a therapeutic word used during my darkest years of distress. I think it would be helpful to share with you some of the characteristics of this joining of my life with God. First, joining with God began with an initial experience. The Holy Spirit came to me and convicted me of my need for Christ. I remember as an eleven-year-old boy asking Christ to be my Savior and to come into my life. It was the beginning of my Christian life. It was the moment the life of God entered into my life. It was the beginning of my spiritual life, the moment of my spiritual birth. It was the first event of my relationship with Christ.

The word "joining" not only pictures an initial connection with Christ but also portrays a continuous abiding with Christ. Christ came into my life not for a visit but for a residency. Robbins helped me to understand that the way I became a Christian was through faith, and the way I became a better Christian was also through faith. I soon discovered that every day of my life should involve an openness to Christ. This daily opening leads Christ's Spirit to produce his character in me. Only the Holy Spirit can produce Christlike qualities. These qualities have been called the "fruit of the Spirit" in Galatians: "But the fruit of the Spirit is love, joy, peace, patience, kindness, goodness, faithfulness, gentleness, self-control…" (Galatians 5:22-23). All nine of these qualities apply to a believer who opens his or her life continuously to the Spirit's work.

The continuous presence of Christ's Spirit means help is available in any situation. Just before Jesus died, he helped his disciples with his death and their coming absence from him. Christ spoke some informative and comforting words to his disciples in their time of distress: "I will ask the Father, and He will give you another Helper, so that He may be with you forever" (John 14:16). Great truths appear in Jesus's words. Notice the word "another." It means another of the same kind with Jesus. In other words, Jesus told his disciples that he was going to return in the Holy Spirit. Notice also the word "helper." It comes from the Greek word *paraclete*, which means "one called alongside to help." The disciples had the assurance that they would receive help in any kind of situation. Finally, notice the expression "be with you forever." The Holy Spirit is a continuous presence in the believer's life.

In addition to the actions of joining and uniting, I also began the act of lamenting. When I saw the note from my wife on the kitchen table, "I have decided to leave," I immediately went into shock. I did not know what to do or what to say. I thought to myself, "This is not real." The shock of the situation put me in denial and unbelief. As time passed, I accepted the reality of the note and moved to great sorrow and even depression. I cried and cried for days and months. At times, I cried for so long that I had no more tears left. It was the only way I knew how to express my profound sorrow. Deep within me, I felt that there was a deeper way to express my sadness. How could I live out my faith in prolonged seasons of pain? How could I live in closeness to God when I hurt so badly?

In my sorrow, a great help came from another one of my seminary professors. He had an amazing knowledge of the Hebrew Bible and a kind spirit both inside and outside the classroom. Several years after I graduated from seminary, I became a teacher and a colleague with my former professor. I moved to campus, and I lived two houses down from him. We entered another dimension of our relationship—talking about our yard work, about working on our cars, about family situations, and many other topics. Over the years we shared a lot of our lives, especially our hurts. He shared with me about a rebellious daughter, and I shared my deep sorrow over my departed wife. We became what Carlyle Marney called "priests to each other."

One day I saw my professor in his yard, and I needed to talk. I spoke frankly about my great sorrow and the flow of my tears. I said, "I need a better way to express my sorrow." The professor said, "There is a better way." Drawing from his own chronic pain and years of knowledge of the Old Testament, he said, "Harold, you need to recover a lost ancient resource for people of faith. It is the practice of lament."

The professor suggested that I start the theory and practice of lament by reading and studying the lament psalms, all forty-five of them. He taught me that laments are not outbursts of unrestrained speech but honest feelings expressing our own words in the context of our faith. He made it known that lamenting was not venting complaints for the sake of complaining. I did study all forty-five of these psalms. I found that they have a methodical cadence that helps to restore order in the midst of disorientation. My friend predicted that learning to lament over my problems would take me deeper than the act of mere crying. Lament represents the honest cry of a hurting heart wrestling with the paradox of pain and the promise of God's goodness. Somewhere in my study of lament, I found this definition: "Lament is a prayer in pain that leads to trust." The lament psalms are written for the space between our brokenness and God's mercy.

My professor made it explicitly clear that my investigation into the lament psalms was not just an educational experience. It was an exercise in personal lament to help me with my deep sorrow. The Hebrew people viewed lament as a gift of God. That is the reason they included them in their hymnal. I desperately needed help with my sorrow. I was caught by circumstances in an in-between time or a state of ambiguity, and as a result I felt displaced, confused, frustrated, and angry. So, with the help of my friend and his recommendation of readings on lament, I began the pursuit of learning to lament in the likeness of the Hebrew people of faith.

Before I began the practice of lament, I felt that I needed to know more. I learned that lament means pouring out one's thoughts and feelings, all of them, both positively and negatively. It means bringing our sorrows to God. If we do not lament, we can creep into silence, bitterness, and anger. I also learned that lament is prayer loaded with theology. Belief in God's mercy, redemption, and sovereignty guides our lament. It is precisely because of our beliefs about who God is and what God has done in the past that we bring our complaints to the Lord. Mere complaining is not lament; lamenting involves complaining in the context of faith in God. Lament stands in the gap between human pain and God's promises. The space between our brokenness and God's mercy is where the prayers of lament meet. Lament invites us to turn toward the promises of God while we are still in pain.

Learning to lament gave me permission to cry as well as to express my disappointments to God. I had to unlearn some of what my Southern religion and culture taught me. People in my culture frowned on doubting, complaining to God, and crying. Many of the people in my culture labeled crying as a sign of a lack of faith. They called for stoic resolve to show faith through unflinching, joyful acceptance of my sorrow as God's will. My growth in the study of Scripture led me to trust in God and, in doing so, to feel hopelessness, doubt, and even anger with God at times. Thankfully, my academic pilgrimage helped me to unlearn some things and to learn that I could be honest with God.

I decided to learn to practice lament. I studied all forty-five of the lament psalms. My professor told me to pay attention to the form and movement of these psalms. Most of the lament psalms follow a pattern as God takes grieving people on a journey. According to Stacey Geddiesmith, the poetical odyssey usually includes four key elements: an address to God, a complaint, a request, and an expression of trust and/or praise.[2] I thought it would be a good idea for me to journal the experiences of my lament. So I purchased a journal notebook and recorded my laments. They filled two pages in the journal. The writing was not lengthy, but it expressed the four key elements proposed by Geddiesmith. I interpreted Scripture, and of course I ventilated my feelings in all of my entries. I began with Psalm 13, and I plan to use this psalm to show you how I learned to lament. After my first journal experience using the psalmist's feelings, I proceeded to use the same procedure with many other lament psalms. Four movements in Psalm 13 helped me greatly.

The four movements of Psalm 13 helped me learn how to organize my lament. The first stanza of the psalm involves the psalmist's address to God. His crisis of disorientation evokes a question to God: "How long, LORD?" (13:1). Notice the name the writer uses for God—"LORD" (*Yahweh*). This name describes God as a God who is personal to human beings. The psalmist begins his lament with the Lord who knows him and will listen to him. Every one of my personal journals began with an acknowledgment of God. This psalm showed me the beauty of pushing my heart toward God in my pain. I admit that my pain was filled with strenuous struggles, deep suffering, and tough questions, but I resolved that even with these feelings I could talk with God. Lament began with a desire to turn to God and pray even while I was in pain.

The second stanza of Psalm 13 states the psalmist's complaints to God (13:1b–2). He asks the question "How long?" four times. The first "How long?" in verse 1 asks if God is going to forget him forever. Then the psalmist asks, "How long will You hide Your face from me?" (13:1b). The psalmist feels deserted by God. This second "How long?" in verse 1 has to do with the psychological effects of God's perceived absence. Third, the psalmist asks, "How long am I to feel anxious in my soul, With grief in my heart all the day?" (13:2a). The precise nature of the psalmist's pain is ambiguous. It could be physical, emotional, spiritual, or a combination of any and all of these. It is certain, though, that the writer hurts all day long, every day. The fourth and final "How long?" reveals that the psalmist has an enemy. Some Old Testament writers think the psalmist was sick, and death loomed as an enemy. "How long will my enemy be exalted over me?" (13:2b). The enemy seems to be getting the upper hand, eager to proclaim victory over the psalmist. It sounds as if the psalmist is sick almost to death.

I had to learn that I could complain to God. I had many dissatisfactions, but I kept them mainly to myself. As my pain journey continued, I ventured in my journaling to complain. I complained about my marital breakup. Later, I complained about the physical and emotional turmoil brought on by the cancers. I moved slowly from acknowledging God to sharing my complaints with God.

In the third stanza (13:3–4), the psalmist turns from complaint to making requests to God. Requests in the lament psalms commonly follow or are interlaced among the complaints. The psalmist first requests the Lord to move from absence to presence: "Consider and answer me, O LORD my God" (13:3a). Instead of forgetting, he wants God to remember him and answer him. He then requests for God's restoration of him: "Enlighten my eyes, or I will sleep the sleep of death" (13:3b). This request asks for the sparkle to return to his eyes, which have been dimmed by grief and pain—the sparkle of health and healing that can only come through the restoration of the psalmist's relationship with God. If God does not "enlighten his eyes," then his eyes will close in the sleep of death, and the enemy will have the victory. The psalmist thinks God must respond out of God's goodness. The writer's language intends to touch God's heart with every plausible idea or argument that might make a difference.

My complaints led naturally to requests for God to respond to my situations. I pled with God to mend our marriage. I asked God to forgive me where I had failed. In the episodes with cancer, I asked God to give negative results for my body scans. I asked for peace and comfort during the turmoil of chemo treatment. Lament kept me turning toward trust by giving me words to fill the wilderness between painful reality and hopeful longings.

The fourth stanza of Psalm 13 begins with a transition—"But I." It is a movement in the lament hymn that points to a different outcome. The theme of this stanza is the decision to express and to praise: "But I have trusted in Your faithfulness; my heart shall rejoice in Your salvation" (13:5). The psalmist expresses his trust in the faithfulness of God. God is trustworthy. People can trust God. The psalmist can trust not only God's faithfulness but also God's work of redemption. Time and time again, God rescues God's people. Suffering does not mean God has forgotten or abandoned God's people. We can decide to trust God and know God's gracious plan is being worked out, even if we cannot see it.

The psalmist ends his hymn in stanza 4 with praise: "I will sing to the LORD, because He has looked after me" (13:6). Throughout the psalms of lament, there is a destination of trust. Through all the pain, questions, hurts, and injustices, the psalmist's lament leads to an experience of worship. Lament is God's way of shaping our attitudes and perceptions so that we can learn to lament in the right things. Lament turns our hearts so we can sing about God's grace.

Though no one taught me how to cry, the steps of lament had to be taught to me by others. Each problem brought a new lament, and each lament followed the same journey: acknowledging the reality of God, complaining to God about my situation, making requests to God for help, and closing with confidence in God and praise of God. The journey of lament took me through the pains while clinging to my faith in God. While lament is a journey, the great news is that I do not walk in my own strength. It is not simply a matter of our determination and willpower. Instead, God helps us to keep trusting through the pain.

After I finished every lament over my suffering, I wondered whether the storm would be over. The end of a lament does not mean we will then sail on a placid sea. The storm may continue to rage, but in the midst of the storm, there is a reassuring presence. Complaint and trust, pain and joy, may coexist. Because the psalmist believed in the steadfast love of God, he was driven to protest and to question when his experience seemed to be pointing in another direction. Godly lament does not signal a lack of trust, and trust does not prevent lament. I found that my belief in God's steadfast love and my debilitating weariness, pain, and joy represented strange partners, yet from my faith in God, hope remained firm. I lamented for a reason—to express my genuine sorrow to God. Studying the lament psalms and writing and verbalizing my own lament did more than tears could do for me. It helped me gain a God-ordained perspective and live with pain and praise simultaneously.

A fifth good help for our pain is the exercise of enduring. A simple life experience taught me a valuable lesson in getting help for my pain. I was in a church in Kansas City, Missouri, teaching a Bible study. It was a time of great distress in my life. The pastor sensed my hurt, so he treated me to lunch each day, coupled with long, caring conversations. One day he wanted to show me the sights of Kansas City. One place we visited was the Hallmark Headquarters. The cards were printed in a large building, and on the side of the building was a Hallmark retail store with all kinds of cards and posters. I enjoyed looking at the vast display of cards and reading the messages inside them. After strolling around the room where the cards were kept, I went into a room filled with posters. One poster caught my attention immediately. It was the picture of a cat hanging on a tree limb by his front paws. Somehow the creator of the poster put a frightened look on the cat's face. The words underneath the picture read: "Hang in there, Baby!" The picture communicated to me that in the midst of my troubles, I need to hang in there, to endure. I bought the poster. I put it on the wall of my office. It is a constant reminder that I need to persevere through my pain and problems.

A prominent word in the New Testament that is translated "endure" is *hupomeno*. It is the combination of two Greek words—*hupo*, meaning "under," and *meno*, meaning "to remain." These two words together mean "to endure under the load." The word is translated as "be patient," "persevere," "endure," and "be steadfast." Life brings us heavy loads—personal struggles, family problems, illnesses, and many others. The apostle Paul wrote, "God is faithful, so He will not allow you to be tempted beyond what you are able, but with the temptation will provide the way of escape also, so that you will be able to endure it" (1 Corinthians 10:13b). The word "temptation" could be translated "trials." Paul said that God will not let us face trials beyond our ability but will make a way out so that we can endure. The way out is not an exit from a hardship but a means of making it through a hardship. If we are faithful, God will enable us to endure.

Patience or endurance comes as a fruit of the Spirit: "But the fruit of the Spirit is…patience" (Galatians 5:22). We cannot endure all of life's challenges without help; human fortitude does not produce endurance—the Spirit does. Christian patience is not a grim acceptance of hardships. It is waiting when nothing seems to be happening and when all the circumstances seem calculated to bring only discouragement. Patience is God's nature. God refuses to give up hope for the world. Believers need to reproduce God's undefeatable patience during difficult seasons of life.

The Spirit does not give patience or steadfastness without a human choice. Believers need to want the fruit of the Spirit. When we open our lives to the Spirit, fruit will come. In the movie *Chariots of Fire*, Eric Liddell is preparing to run the four-hundred-meter race, and one of the other runners hands him a note of support, quoting 1 Samuel 2:30: "He who honors Me I will honor." Liddell wins the race and receives a gold medal. During the race, Liddell talks to himself and to God. He realizes that he must depend on God and run with all his might.[3]

God's patience is attainable for human beings. Let me share three examples of people enduring under the heavy load of troubles. Job survived under his suffering, maintaining spiritual integrity and waiting patiently for the Lord to transform his situation. He is remembered in the book of James: "We count those blessed who endured. You have heard of the endurance of Job and have seen the outcome of the Lord's dealings, that the Lord is full of compassion and is merciful" (James 5:13). By God's strength, Job endured under his trials. He lost his material goods; his children died in a storm; he lost his health. It would seem that Job was overloaded with life's burdens. But he kept on during and after each episode of distress. Job's example provides encouragement for the attitude of endurance.

The trait of patience used as steadfastness appears throughout the life and ministry of Jesus Christ. He endured the limitations and hardships of being human. He continued to do the work of the heavenly Father despite criticisms and rejection. He faced death with courage. He endured the terrible suffering of crucifixion, persisting until his death. Three days later Jesus arose from the grave, and forty days later he ascended to the Father. What a tremendous example of endurance incarnated in the life, death, and resurrection of Jesus!

A third example of endurance is Paul, the apostle. After his conversion from Judaism, he experienced rejection and persecution from the Jews. Let me remind you of some of Paul's hardships: ". . . beaten times without number, often in danger of death. Five times I received from the Jews thirty-nine lashes. Three times I was beaten with rods, once I was stoned, three times I was shipwrecked, a night and a day I have spent adrift at sea" (2 Corinthians 11:23–25). Despite all of Paul's hardships, he remained steadfast. He even said, ". . .we do not lose heart" (2 Corinthians 4:1b).

These examples gave me the inspiration for "hanging in there." I remember some of my experiences when I walked in the darkness of distress. I practiced reflective thinking. Life's hardships created a feeling of being trapped in darkness. Glimmers of light came when I looked back on my theological training, my teachings in church, and my personal quiet times with God. When I thought of those great memories, they helped me get through the darkness.

In addition to my reflective thinking, I practiced a lot of self-talk. Many of those conversations were self-corrections. When I developed negative thoughts, I felt it was time to say something to myself. I reprimanded myself for my negativity and urged myself to move to more positive thinking. These talks often helped me correct my attitude. When I faced hard situations such as chemo treatments and their side effects, I did not want to do them. But many times I told myself, "You can take these treatments." On a few occasions I had to tell myself that I was not going to die. I said to myself, "You will get through this and will be alive tomorrow!" Many times I had to say, "I can get through this divorce. I am not going to let it destroy me." Lest I am misunderstood, I assure you that my ability to "hang in there" did not come from human effort alone. It came from the presence and the strength of the Spirit as I yielded to God's presence with me.

I got help for my hurts in many places and from many people. It was good help, but the best help I received for my pain came from God. I prayed honestly and persistently; I opened my life to the indwelling Christ continuously; I learned to lament at times; and I endured because of Christ's presence and strength working through my willingness.

## Notes

[1] Andrew Murray, *With Christ in the School of Prayer* (New Kensington, PA: Whitaker House, 1981).

[2] Stacey Geddiesmith, "'My God, My God, Why?' Understanding the Lament Psalms," *Reformed Worship*, June 2010, quoted in Mark Vroegop, *Dark Clouds—Deep Mercy: Discovering the Grace of Lament* (Wheaton, Illinois: Crossway, 2019), 29.

[3] *Chariots of Fire*, directed by Hugh Hudson, written by Colin Welland, produced by David Puttnam, released October 9, 1981.

# Chapter 7

# Surprising Profits

Educators use the word "assessment" in evaluating a school's educational program. Throughout my forty-three years of teaching, I participated in numerous assessments. School administrators circulated a course evaluation form near the end of each semester. Students had the opportunity to evaluate their courses as well as the professors who taught those courses. I learned from these appraisals, which contained both positive and negative comments. I did receive positive strokes from students, including "makes the class interesting," "emphasizes the relevance of the material," and "organizes his lectures in an understandable manner." Before my pride becomes too prominent, I also need to say that I received negative evaluations about the course content as well as my teaching style. Some comments were "talks too fast," "uses words he assumes we know," "cannot read clearly what he writes on the board," and "gives hard tests." From these and other negative comments, I adjusted my speaking rate and my word usage, sought to improve my writing on the board, and had a few fellow educators evaluate my tests.

No teacher is perfect. No matter how long one teaches, students will share both positive and negative feelings. The positive comments encouraged me. The negative comments gave me a new perception to consider. When I first received student evaluations, I loved the positive feedback, but I did not like the negative comments. In fact, I disagreed with most of them. Thankfully, colleagues helped me navigate and learn from the negative comments. Over the years, assessment became an important and helpful exercise. I never wanted to punctuate my teaching with a period, that is, think that it was good enough. I learned to punctuate my teaching with a comma, paying close attention to every positive and negative evaluation. There is always room for growth and improvement.

Assessments do not just occur within schools, businesses, and other organizations. Individual evaluations happen constantly with life experiences. We assess a lot of what happens to us as good, and we assess some of what happens to us as bad. Think about a few life events: We get an excellent health report. We earn a job promotion and a substantial salary increase. Parents have their first child. Students are chosen for a scholarship. How do we evaluate these kinds of experiences? I have found that life is good, but it is not all good. Consider these experiences: We have an accident, and serious injury results. We receive a notice that our job has been eliminated. A friend betrays us. A parent has Alzheimer's disease and needs constant care. A heart attack happens. We are diagnosed with leukemia. How do we evaluate these kinds of experiences? Of course, we think they are bad, and we cannot see any profit in them. And all of us prefer the good over the bad. We expect life to be smooth, but there are bumps in every life.

Just as the negative comments helped me to become a better teacher, the bad things that happen to us can help us become better people. When numerous distresses came into my life—a marital break and five cancers—at first, I could see nothing but bad. But as I walked the road of pain and read Scripture, talked with people in pain, and engaged in introspective thinking, the bad things began to take on a profitable note. It took time to see the profit of my pain. I dealt with my problems academically and spiritually. I had to take many backward looks as well as project many forward hopes. I want to share with you five profitable benefits from my pain.

First, my suffering drove me closer to God. On many occasions, I felt I had reached the end of my strength and the limits of my knowledge, and I knew I needed greater help. In the King James Version of Psalm 107:27, the psalmist describes sailors who "are at their wit's end." The psalm begins with descriptions of an experience at sea: "They…go down to the sea in ships, that do business in great water" (verse 23). Then the writer relates how the sailors come up against the fury and might of the sea. The winds blow, the storm comes, and the ship is tossed in the large waves. The weather becomes so intense and severe that the sailors reel and stagger from the pitching and rolling of the vessel. They are at their wit's end.

What happens when we are at our wit's end? It means that we are at the end of both our human knowledge and our human strength. We are at the end of our human resources. We have gotten as far as our abilities and capabilities can take us. What then is beyond our wit's end? Of course, God is greater than our human intellect and power. The sailors in the psalm reached out to God: "Then they cried out to the LORD in their trouble, And He brought them out of their distresses" (Psalm 107:28). God's resources are beyond our distress. The crisis of the storm drove the sailors to God. It is right to pray when we are at the end of ourselves. It is, of course, not right to pray in an emergency and then to stop praying after the crisis. Coming to God in a crisis needs to keep us continuing to pray in gratitude to God and in constant search of God's guidance afterward. But it is certainly profitable to pray at one's wit's end. When we pray, our minds are stilled and quieted. When we pray, our hearts are warmed, and life is not cold intellect. When we pray to God in a crisis, help may come from another human being. God may lead someone to us to help us.

Suffering drives many people to God. It does not drive everyone, for some choose to live by their own strength and wisdom. But for some, this suffering becomes the occasion of their initial experience with the Lord. They become a Christian as a result of the push of their crisis and the pull of the Spirit of God.

I became a Christian at the age of eleven. No serious distress forced me to seek God. My relationship with God came as a result of Sunday school teachers, pastors, and my parents. I had a personal experience with God, but I had no idea that my experience would become greater. When my marital separation happened and the cancers came, I arrived at my wit's end. I felt that God would be with me and would help me through my crises. God was and God did. God was present with me at my eleven-year-old conversion and at my forty-six-year-old relational break. From age eleven to forty-six, I sensed the presence of God in my life. But at forty-six I drew nearer to God because of my crises. God was always present, though I did not feel this presence at times.

I learned that if I drew near to God, God would draw near to me (see James 4:8). I can begin to describe what I learned about God during the dark nights of my soul. I learned that God is full of acceptance and grace. God will never refuse me drawing near. God never stands away from me but always draws near. In God's closeness, I learned of God's love and grace. God loves me no matter what I do. The distresses of my life disturbed me greatly, but they never destroyed my belief that God loves and cares for me. In our close companionship, I learned that God is far more interested in my spiritual character than my physical comfort. God is much more concerned about my needs than my wants. My closer walk with the Lord has caused me to abandon the "Cosmic Santa Claus" concept to one of a loving God.

I never did get so close to God that I attained perfection. I continued to neglect God and disobey God with my thoughts, words, and actions. But I learned during those imperfect times about the mercy and forgiveness of God. In Jesus' story of the man who had two sons, he told about one son who rebelled against the father and left for the far country. But when this son came to himself and decided to go home and asked to be made a servant, the father saw him, ran to meet him, embraced him, and celebrated his homecoming. He also gave him a ring to symbolize the fact that the father welcomed him as a son and not a slave. (See Luke 15.) If we turn to God in humble dependence and admit our need, coming as a child, we will always find God waiting to receive us and treat us as a child. Cancer, divorce, and other distresses brought me to a closer walk with the Lord, and getting closer to God gave me a greater love and admiration for God. I was not smart enough to negotiate my way through troubles. I was not strong enough to take what life handed me. So my first positive assessment of pain was that it brought me closer to God.

Strange as it may seem, suffering has the possibility of generating other positive assessments. Hardships are not always profitable for those who never escape the idea that pain and suffering can only be bad. I stayed in a negative mood early in my hurts. But as time passed and I sought God's help, God showed me the ways my pain could be profitable. Deep thinking, helpful friends, and testimonies of people going through pain also helped me. I found that pain helped develop a Christian character.

My positive evaluations came primarily from an experience with James 1:2–12. In my teaching schedule one semester, the time had come for me to teach the letter of James in my New Testament class. I reviewed the context of the book and began in James 1 to study every word and its original meaning. I then began to interpret what the words mean to people in today's world. On this occasion of preparation, reading and studying James brought a new light to the text. In addition to me interpreting the text, the text also interpreted me and my trials.

James wrote about trials in 1:2–12. The word translated "trial"—*peirosmos*—and its verbal cognate—*peirazo*—are important for us to understand.

The words have two distinct meanings in the New Testament. They can denote either an outward trial or process testing, or the inner enticement to sin—"temptation." The context of *peirosmos* in James 1:2 refers to any difficulty that may threaten us: physical illness, financial reversal, relationship problems, the death of a loved one. The context of James 1:2–12 seems to be that James was thinking primarily of outward afflictions.

The ordinary response to the inevitable troubles of life is anger, resentment, irritability, or despondency. But James called for Christians to adjust their attitudes to these trials: "Consider it all joy, my brothers and sisters, when you encounter various trials" (James 1:2). The verb tense in verse 2 implies a decisive action in harnessing a joyful attitude. C. Leslie Mitton translates this verse as "Make up your mind to regard adversities as something to welcome and be glad about."[1] The word "joy" is one of the big words of the New Testament. When God controls a human life and, by the living presence of the Holy Spirit, brings a person's heart and will into obedience, the consequence of that life is joy. Trials can become occasions to bring this joy.

After calling for an attitude adjustment in verse 2, James moves to some reasons for wanting this joy: ". . . the testing of your faith produces endurance. And let endurance have its perfect result, so that you may be perfect and complete, lacking in nothing" (1:3–4). The "testing" of our faith is a necessary condition for its development. There is no way of knowing whether our faith is growing except by meeting and surviving trials, proving that our faith does not fail. The outcome of the adversities that test our faith, provided it does not fail under them, is described as "endurance"—a steadfast faithfulness in trying times. The testing of our faith is not intended to determine whether we have faith or not; it is intended to purify faith that already exists. The etymology of the word "endurance" points to the concept of "remaining under." Christians learn to remain under God's direction over the long haul only when they face difficulty.

When faith is tested, then, the immediate result is, or can be, endurance. But, as valuable as it is, endurance itself is not the final goal of testing. The benefits of testing come to believers only when they respond by allowing endurance to do its intended work. What is this "perfect result" that endurance is intended to achieve? James seems to communicate that a person remains under their load of trials until they have grown or matured.

The concept of Christian maturity and growth through suffering is part of the message of the New Testament. James stresses that it calls believers to a magnificent reality, noting that the tragedies and troubles of life are to be met with joyful awareness and that the path of Christian character is not measured by deliverance from suffering but by the believer being redeemed in it so they will be "lacking in nothing."

Suffering highlights to me that God has not created me for independent living. Pain moved me in a vertical direction toward God, but it also moved me in a horizontal direction toward hurting people. My hurt moved me to help others with the same pain I was experiencing. The strong, independent, self-made person is a delusion. Everyone in pain needs help. I have been helped by other people sharing their pain with me. Suffering is a messenger telling us that to be human is to be "priests to each other."

During my pain, many people in pain reached out to me, and I cried to people for help with my pain. These people helped me walk through some tough times. God became known through others who shared God's grace with me. Paul David Tripp helped me to see that "God's people are to be the countenance of his face, the touch of his hand, the sound of his voice, the evidence of his love, the picture of his presence, and the demonstration of his faithfulness."[2] God has blessed believers with an outstanding, healing community to help those who hurt.

When I became a seminary professor in 1976, I was assigned to teach pastoral ministry. I had read a number of books on the subject, and they helped me prepare for the course. But one book that helped me more than all the others was Henri Nouwen's work *The Wounded Healer*.[3] When Nouwen taught prospective ministerial students at Yale Divinity School, he told them to care for other people's wounds but also to make their wounds into an important source of healing. He challenged potential ministers to admit their wounds and then to use them to help others with their wounds. I did not know that getting ready to teach a class of future pastors would prepare me not only to help others but also to find help in my own hurting.

Nouwen got his picture of the wounded healer from the life and ministry of Jesus Christ. He was quite fond of an old legend in the Talmud:

> Rabbi Yoshua ben Levi came upon Elijah the prophet while he was standing at the entrance of Rabbi Simeron be Yohai's cave. …He asked Elijah, "When will the Messiah come?"

Elijah replied, "Go and ask him for yourself."

"Where is he?"

"Sitting at the gates of the city."

"How shall I know him?"

"He is sitting among the poor, covered with wounds. The others unbind all their wounds at the same time and then bind them up again. But he unbinds them one at a time and binds it up again, saying to himself, 'Perhaps I shall be needed. If so, I must always be ready so as not to delay for a moment.'"[4]

Nouwen explained that Christ had given his story a fuller interpretation and significance by making his broken body the means to liberation and new life. Nouwen taught me to care for other people's wounds but also to make their wounds into an important source of healing.

Jesus Christ is the ultimate model for ministry. He had an incredible love for human beings. He devoted lots of time and energy to others during his earthly ministry. Matthew gives a snapshot from Jesus's ministry: "Jesus was going through all the cities and the villages, teaching in their synagogues and proclaiming the gospel of the kingdom, and healing every disease and every sickness. Seeing the crowds, He felt compassion for them" (Matthew 9:35–36a). No one went unnoticed by the Master. He also saw the neglected people of society—blind, lame, sick, demon possessed, and many others. He had care and concern for everyone.

Jesus expected his followers to be like he was in character and to do what he did. He was a wounded healer, and he wanted his followers to be likewise. To help others, we need to be aware of our own weaknesses. Doing well in helping others is not pretending to be strong. The believer's reputation is not honored by publicly faking what isn't privately true. My greatest help in supporting others came when I shared my experiences of life with an alcoholic father, a heartbreaking divorce, and the pain of five cancers. I learned that little good happened when I denied weakness, and all kinds of good happened when I confessed it. I recognized that I had been wounded and many others had also, and my pain gave me a unique opportunity to help others who were hurting.

Because of what I had gone through, I knew what would be helpful and what would not be helpful. I learned when to speak and when to listen. I knew what it was to feel helpless. My pain provided an excellent resource for me to be an agent of God's comfort in the lives of sufferers. God does not want me to hoard my suffering; God wants me to share it with others who are in pain. I do hope that I have imitated Jesus's ministry. I know I have been helped when God used other people to help me.

My pilgrimage with pain presented me with many challenges. One of the traits that needed changing in my life was discontentment. Up until my middle years, I was basically a satisfied person. But numerous episodes happened to me in those middle years. I began to notice my disposition change from contentment to discontentment, and the signs of discontentment became noticeable not only to me but also to my friends. In my marital breakup, I began to feel as if I were a failure in life. I became guilty over the fact that I might have hurt another person and not lived up to being a good partner in marriage. I saw happy married people and remembered those days in my life, becoming resentful of my new single status. I felt that such a time would never come again. Life was turning sour for me, and I was headed straight to the pit of bitterness if something did not change.

Signs of discontentment also came during my time with cancers. Every diagnosis brought disappointment, self-rejection, a troubled spirit, and negative feelings. Anxiety and fear pursued me in every diagnosis and treatment. I began to notice an uncomfortable restlessness in my life. Episodes of bitterness visited me, but thankfully these episodes did not become permanent. I became tired of discontent, but discontent seemed to win most days in my life.

I asked numerous times, "How can I move from dissatisfaction to satisfaction? How can I achieve the inner peace that I so desperately want? How can I keep from being a permanently bitter person?" I knew that contentment was a Stoic term meaning "self-sufficiency." The Stoics solved their problems by renouncing negative situations and summoning strength within themselves. I tried hard to renounce my negative circumstances and rid myself of discontentment, but my attempts failed. I had to come to the conclusion that my answer was not within myself. The answer had to come from Someone greater and more powerful than I was.

A study of Paul's letter to the Philippians led me to that Someone—namely, God. Paul gave the secret of his contentment in Philippians 4:11–13. He was in prison in Rome when he wrote this passage, and even though his ministry had been threatened and his living conditions were uncomfortable, he wrote about satisfaction: "Not that I speak from need, for I have learned to be content in whatever circumstances I am. I know how to get along with little, and I also know how to live in prosperity; in any and every circumstance I have learned the secret of being filled and going hungry, both of having abundance and suffering need. I can do all things through Him who strengthens me." Paul testified that he was content in seasons of both abundance and want, sharing with readers that his sovereign independence in all circumstances came from his relationship with Christ.

Paul's words "I have learned the secret" deserve special attention. In Greek, these were technical words often used to describe an initiation into one of the Greek mystery religions. Their initiation opened the revelation of certain mysteries. Paul used the expression to say that he had been initiated into the secret of contentment through his experience with Christ. He did not boast, "I am the captain of my soul." He was not Stoic in his own resources and unmoved by either good times or bad times. Paul considered himself as a person in Christ—the One who strengthened him so he could face life's dangers, privations, relational problems, or illnesses.

Life hands all of us many challenges. One of the hardest tests is for our contentment to win over our discontentment. The words "more," "better," "success," "recognition," "money," and many others upset our equilibrium for peace of mind. We think if we could have more money, recognition from others, great success in our career, a healthy body, and many more cultural values, we would be content. Perhaps nothing challenges inner peace more than suffering. Up until my middle years, I was mostly a satisfied person. Of course, periodical threats to my contentment came and went. But suffering eventually hit me hard, and I became a discontented person. I realized that something needed to happen in life to move me toward contentment.

My contentment during the great period of pain came gradually. I was interrupted in gaining peace by listening to the secular solutions of what it takes to make one happy. Many times I allowed my distressing circumstances to dictate my disposition. More than I care to admit it, I tried the Stoic road to contentment—self-sufficiency. Nothing gave me more poise and peace than the indwelling Christ living in me. The more I submitted to Christ, the more I found inner peace, outward poise, and a more positive attitude. My journey to find contentment has not resulted in a perfect state. I still struggle with discontent, but contentment does come through Christ no matter what I am facing. As I look back over my distressing journey with pain, I can see signs of improvement—not perfection, but progress.

Today I look back and think about the lessons I have learned about contentment during distressing times. I learned that many things happened to me that I could not handle. I could try to be smart or strong, but my efforts never brought genuine contentment and inner satisfaction. Paul's motto of Christ-sufficiency, not self-sufficiency, has made all the difference in my disposition. Looking back, I can see that the indwelling Christ led me to value relationships more than anything on earth. People in my life became more important than material goods, vocational success, and societal recognition. I learned to value my God more. I also grew in the value of my wife, my children, and of course my grandchildren.

Paul taught me that my outward circumstances did not have to dictate my state of mind. I could be rich or poor. I could be well or sick. I could be married or divorced. I could be recognized by others or I could be ignored. No earthly existence determined my contentment. It came from a relationship with Christ.

### Notes

[1] C. Leslie Mitton, *The Epistle of James* (Grand Rapids: Wm. B. Eerdmans Publishing Company, 1966), 20.

[2] Paul David Tripp, *Suffering: Gospel Hope When Life Doesn't Make Sense* (Wheaton, IL: Crossway, 2018), 191.

[3] Henri J. M. Nouwen, *The Wounded Healer: Ministry in Contemporary Society* (Garden City, NY: Doubleday & Company, Inc. 1972).

[4] Quoted in Michael Ford, *Wounded Healer: Portrait of Henri J. M. Nouwen* (New York: Doubleday, 1999), 45.

# Chapter 8

# Ultimate Hope

On December 17, 1927, the USS *S-4*, an eight-year-old submarine, was submerged off the coast of Provincetown, Maine. The Coast Guard destroyer *Paulding* inadvertently collided with *S-4* when it resurfaced. The ship rammed the submarine and punched holes in the sub's hull. Freezing water flowed into the sub and it began to sink.

On the bottom, 110 feet down, *S-4*'s crew scrambled to bring the situation under control. Thirty-four men on board took refuge in the engine room, but the situation deteriorated. Water began to fill the space where the men had gathered, and the tanks that supplied their air began to diminish. The trapped sailors could only hope that the world above was on its way.

Ten Navy divers were rushed to the scene of the accident to begin rescue efforts. Minutes after one diver located the sub, he began tapping on the hull, hoping survivors would respond. The sailors tapped a message to the rescuers: "Hurry!" Later the divers heard a new tapping: the sailors asking, "Is there any hope?" There was none. Seven days after the collision, on December 24, 1927, the Navy reported that all of *S-4*'s men were presumed dead.

When I read that story, it impacted me greatly. The sailors' question impressed me: "Is there any hope?" The word "hope" grabbed my attention. The sailors' hope was to be rescued and to return to their families and Navy personnel. They had a desire for immediate hope. I have no record of any of the sailors communicating about ultimate hope—that is, a desire to live in heaven after their earthly deaths.

Words do not have meanings within themselves. They have usages. How a word is used gives it meaning. The word "hope" in the English language is often used to express wishful thinking. Its usage suggests a desire for something to happen without certainty that it will. Notice how people use the word "hope": "I hope my diagnosis is not cancer." "I hope I catch fish on my next outing." "I hope our team wins the SEC championship." "I hope it doesn't rain so I can mow my lawn." None of these wishes give absolute certainty—only wishful thinking.

On a more serious side of the usage of hope, I have heard people say, "Well, I hope that I am a Christian." Or "I hope that I go to heaven when I die." Notice that neither one of these two statements expresses confidence or certainty. On the basis of the prominent usages of hope in our world, I want to turn to the New Testament to see how the divinely inspired writers used the word. The New Testament word for hope is *elpis*. It was used to express confident certainty based on the promises of God, and we cannot get any more certain than that. When God promises something, we can expect it to happen.

As we face two critical issues of life mentioned above—being a Christian and going to heaven—it seems to me that we need to use the New Testament meaning of hope as confident certainty. God has promised a relationship with us through our faith, and our matter of being a Christian is settled. God has made many promises, but in the main part of our study I want to examine two of them. First, after the end of history or time, God promises a new heaven and a new earth. Second, when a believer dies or the Lord returns, God promises to give them a new body. (See Revelation 21:1–6; 1 Corinthians 15:29–49.) That's the reason I love to sing these words of the popular hymn: "I'm standing on the promises of God."[1] Being a Christian and going to heaven depend on the promises of God.

New Testament hope presents confidence in two spheres of human existence—our present time on earth and our future existence in heaven. The believer's timeline of life may be divided between the hope of the immediate and the hope of the ultimate. When accidents, illnesses, diseases, and other distressing situations happen, believers hold out for God's immediate hope in the present time that includes God's strength and presence. Of course, God allows for healing and rescue in some cases but not in every case. In the present life, we may face no hope for a continued earthly life. A distressing situation may appear to be leading to death. Often I have asked, "What will happen when there is no healing or deliverance from pain in my life?" My immediate hope, as I have written, is God's presence and God's strength during the days of my earthly existence. My ultimate hope is for a new heaven and a new earth as well as a resurrected body. Fortunately, I have confident certainty based on the promises of God that my life after my earthy existence will be better.

Think with me about the desires of human beings. Most people wish for a better world and a better body. Most people I know want healing from diseases and illnesses so they can live longer on earth. They want to live a better life on earth after debilitating accidents. Physical illnesses and serious accidents produce a lot of wishful thinking. Even God's creation has a desire for a better existence. Paul attributed human nature to the inanimate object of nature: "For the creation was subjected to futility, not willingly, but because of Him who subjected it, in hope…" (Romans 8:20). Paul referred to a past event that fell on the natural order following Adam's disobedience. The created order became affected by the Fall, and it needs redemption and restoration. Paul summarizes God's curse on nature with the word "futility." It means emptiness, purposelessness, and temporary existence.

Creation has a desire to be liberated from its futility. God promises change: "that the creation itself also will be set free from its slavery to corruption into the freedom of the glory of the children of God" (Romans 8:21). Paul turned to God's promise for the future of the created order. Its subjection to frustration will not last forever. One day it will have a glorious release from bondage, a redeemed universe. So far, the apostle has told us that creation was subjected to futility and will be liberated in the future. While creation is waiting for this future redemption, Paul attributes another human quality to nature. This time he speaks of creation groaning: "For we know that the whole creation groans and suffers…" (8:22a). Nature earnestly desires God's final redemption. The universe is not going to be destroyed but rather liberated, transformed, and filled with the glory of God. Creation's ultimate desire will be actualized. That is the promise of God.

The word "glory" communicates future redemption of both God's creation and God's children. Both creations are suffering at the present time, and both will ultimately be set free. "For the eagerly awaiting creation waits for the revealing of the sons and daughters of God" (8:19). The word "eagerly" means "to wait with the head raised and the eye fixed on that point of the horizon from which the expected object is to come."[2] It pictures someone standing on tiptoe or stretching the neck, craning forward in order to be able to see. What creation is looking for is the revelation of

God's children, which is the disclosure of their identity as well as their investiture with glory. What Paul meant by creation included the totality of the works of God. These works encompass the earth and all its contents, inanimate and animate. It also includes the heavenly bodies, human beings, and total of subhuman nature. Paul presented the hope that the pains of all creation will be restored from its imperfection and restored to its primal perfection. History is moving to a God-appointed glorious future for the people of God.[3]

The doctrine of the new earth as taught in Scripture is an influential one. It gives us understanding of the life to come for believers. The Bible assures us that God will create a new earth on which believers shall live to God's praise in resurrected bodies. The total work of Christ is nothing less than to redeem his entire creation from the negative effects of sin. That purpose will not be accomplished until God has ushered in a new earth. History ends with a new creation in which rebellion and evil have no part.

Now I want to share with you about this new world to come. This new world is an ultimate hope. A number of Old Testament prophecies speak of a glorious future for the earth. They tell us that at some time in the future, the earth will be more productive than it is now. The desert shall blossom as the rose, the plowman shall overtake the reaper, and the mountains shall drop sweet wine. They tell us that the sound of weeping will no longer be heard on the earth (Revelation 21:4). They tell us that on the new earth the wolf and the lamb shall feed together (Isaiah 65:25), and the earth shall be full of the knowledge of the Lord as waters cover the sea (Habakkuk 2:14).

The most extensive and descriptive picture of the eternal blessedness of God's people in the new heaven and the new earth appears in Revelation 21:1–22:6. The writer of Revelation, known as John, elaborates on the promise God gave long ago to Isaiah that God would "create new heavens and a new earth" (Isaiah 65:17). The writer begins with a general introduction to the new creation in Revelation 21:1: "Then I saw a new heaven and a new earth; for the first heaven and the first earth passed away, and there is no longer any sea." The Greek word for "new" designated something that already exists but now appears in a new or fresh aspect—in this case, an already existing heaven and earth that become completely transformed. It is the same world but gloriously rejuvenated. The expression "new heavens and a new earth" constitutes the totality of natural creation. The newness of new heavens and a new earth does not mean a creation totally different from the present one; it means the creation of a new earth that, though it has been gloriously renewed, stands in continuity with the present one. The sea, which was a symbol of separation, isolation, and rebellious power set against God, will disappear from the new earth.

The centerpiece of the new heaven and earth is the new Jerusalem. It is the holy city, prepared as a bride adorned for her husband (21:2). That is to say, the city originated in heaven and is beautiful beyond all comparison. Obviously, the writer was not referring to the rebuilding of the earthly city of Jerusalem. He sees a new Jerusalem. It is qualitatively different from the old Jerusalem. In the Hebrew Bible, Jerusalem is the special city where God dwells with God's people. In referencing the new Jerusalem, the writer envisions a new community and a new way that God dwells with God's people.

The writer hears a loud voice from the throne: "Behold, the tabernacle of God is among the people, and He will dwell among them, and they shall be His people, and God Himself will be among them" (Revelation 21:3). Revelation depicts life in this redeemed city. God's people find their real blessing in union with God and in the realization of God's presence with them. This real and perfect fellowship with God eliminates sorrow, pain, and death from their lives. The things pertaining to the first heaven and earth have been completely eliminated. This is a picture of the original creation fully restored in redemption (21:5). God changes the old into the new. God is on the throne, that is, God has the sovereign power to design and complete a new earth. God commanded John to write because the truth of the revelation is accurate. What God has revealed about a new creation has been done, is being done, and eventually will be completed. The struggles of the old order are merely the birth pangs of the new creation.

Apparently, God continues to speak. God's words are recorded in Revelation 21:5–8, affirming what the heavenly voice in 21:4 said. "Write, for these words are faithful and true" (21:5). God announces that the goal of the new creation has been accomplished. All things have been transformed by the sovereign power of God. The One who started the process of creation (the Alpha) is the same one who has brought the new creation to its conclusion (the Omega). God said, "It is done" (21:6). The promises and purposes of God are accomplished. The long process will be brought to culmination. All of God's transcendence and greatness are used to help God's creatures. God is the bountiful giver: "I will give water to the one who thirsts from the spring of the water of life, without cost. The ones who overcomes shall inherit these things, and I will be his God, and he will be My son" (21:6b–7). God's grace, which was expressed on earth, becomes even more amazing in the new world.

Revelation 21:8 stands in sharp contrast to the first seven verses of chapter 21. The ones in this verse are followers of evil. Eight epithets are used to describe those who preclude themselves from the kingdom of God. There is no place for them in the holy city. Notice the ones excluded: "the cowardly, and unbelieving, and abominable, and murderers, and sexually immoral persons, and sorcerers, and idolaters, and all liars" (21:8a). These represent those with character traits and behaviors inconsistent with the kingdom of God.

At this point, John expands his initial announcement concerning the new Jerusalem, and he presents an elaborate description of the heavenly city (Revelation 21:9–22:5). John does not depict people somewhere off in space plucking harps and flitting from cloud to cloud. These are God's redeemed people living in community on God's new heaven and earth. John was carried away in the Spirit to a high mountain in order to get a better vision of "the holy city, Jerusalem, coming down out of heaven from God" (21:10). This indicates that the city comes from God. It is not merely a voluntary association of men and women. This beloved community is portrayed as both bride (21:9) and city (21:10–14). What follows in Revelation 21:9–27 is a description of the city and its magnificence, where the author presents a vision of heaven in a tapestry of symbolism that describes God's people triumphant in their perfected and eternal glory.[4]

In Revelation 21:2, John does not describe the new Jerusalem as a city with foundations, walls, and streets, but as a city of people. The new Jerusalem symbolizes redeemed human beings. The expression "coming down out of heaven from God" emphasizes its origin and source. The new city is not something given by human beings; it is something given by God. The likeness of "a bride adorned for her husband" stresses the sacred bond between God and God's people. The redeemed in the new city enjoy the most intimate relationship with God and God's people. John writes about the city "having the glory of God. Her brilliance was like a very valuable stone, like a stone of crystal-clear jasper" (21:11). God's presence radiates throughout the city and in God's people.

In Revelation 21:12–24, Jerusalem is described as beautiful, strong, and ideal. The holy city has a high wall that is emblematic of its security and peace. It is impregnable. Around the wall, there are twelve gates, each made of pearl. They indicate complete and perfect admission into the city. The city is accessible to all of the world, symbolized by three gates on the north, three on the south, three on the east, and three on the west.

The angel who had been talking to John "had a gold measuring rod to measure the city, its gates, and its wall" (Revelation 21:15). The city is thousand stadia or 2,250,000 square miles. This vast perfect cube, patterned after the holy of holies, symbolizes the perfect harmony, symmetry, completeness, and vastness of the glorified church. In this vast holy city, there is sufficient room for every man, woman, and child of every nation, race, people, and tongue. The wall that surrounds the city is 144 cubits, which is the square of 12. The walls symbolize the security and largeness of the city. Furthermore, the city is pure gold like clear glass. John as a poet uses material figures to express spiritual truth, like the splendor of precious stones, pure transparent gold, and magnificent pearls to communicate the glory of the holy city. John uses this brilliant assemblage of colors to portray the majesty of God being exhibited in various attributes of wisdom, justice, and mercy (Rev 21:18–21).

The further John goes to describe the holy city, the more wonderful it becomes. The reader may be surprised that John describes heaven without a temple: "I saw no temple in it" (21:22). There is no temple or sanctuary in the holy city, for in one respect, the city itself is a sanctuary. Its dimension is like the holy of holies in the tabernacle of old. The temple in the new city is no longer a reserved place entered only by the high priest once a year. The continuous open gates convey the idea of perfect freedom of access and fellowship with God. There is no need for the sun or the moon to shine on it, because the presence of God illuminates the city. The city is flooded with the brilliance of God's presence; therefore, darkness of every kind is banished forever.

The holy city has a universal appeal. Isaiah predicted that the nations would be gathered together in Jerusalem under the reign of the Messiah (Isaiah 66:12). John says Isaiah's predictions have been fulfilled: the gathering together of all nations in the holy city. The "kings of the earth" find their true purpose in ministering to the needs of humanity. The new city is inhabited by the redeemed people of God, and they are the "light of the world." In John's vision, the city has no walls to depict its safety, and the gates are always open, signifying admission. In the holy city "coming down out of heaven," the unclean and false may never enter. Only the redeemed can enter the holy city (Revelation 21:27).

The next paragraph (Revelation 22:1–5) should have been included in chapter 21. The paragraph concludes John's description of the holy city. It is reminiscent of the Garden of Eden (Genesis 2:9). It is a place where a river runs and where flowers of refreshment and healing abound. The water is sufficient for all needs. In this picturesque symbolism, John communicates that the redeemed have entered a full, meaningful, and abundant life that they will experience forever. In the holy city, they have been changed from the Adam state of death into the Christ state of eternal life.

John directs the reader's attention to the most important feature of all: namely, that the throne of God and of the Lamb will be in the heavenly Jerusalem, and "His bond-servants will serve Him; they will see His face, and His name will be on their foreheads" (Revelation 22:3b). To see the face of God means more than a look at God. It means to comprehend and understand God. God's name on the "foreheads" of the people means that God's character will reside in all the people in the holy city.

In the beginning of the world, God created the heavens and the earth. God's creation became disrupted by human rebellion, but God promised to redeem the broken situation. At the end of history, we learn about the new heavens and the new earth, which will surpass in splendor anything that humans have seen before. In this new world, there is an intimacy to be constantly enjoyed between God and human beings. The barriers that have separated God and humans will be removed. God's authority will be recognized by everyone, and everything will be done for God. The goal for and the essence of creation will be realized in the new world. Someday God's people will cast all their crowns before God, and we shall be filled with wonder and praise.

Having looked at the new world, we will now turn our attention to the believer's new body. I have lived for more than eight decades on planet earth. My years have been filled with joy and sorrow, agony and ecstasy. I confess that the majority of my life has been enjoyable. I have enjoyed many years of wellness but also a number of years of sickness. I think the good times have outweighed the bad times in my life. I enjoyed my town, a loving family, a challenging education, numerous friends, church, and the pleasures of fishing and watching different sports.

But all through my life I have known what it is to have a frail body. Early in life, measles, mumps, chicken pox, common colds, and influenza invaded my body. I have had numerous cuts and scrapes. I broke my arm and my ankle in high school. My episodes with cancer taught me more about how brittle my body can be. Emotional distresses and relational problems also showed me how vulnerable I am to frail situations. These bumps along the road of life have caused me to long for a well body and mind as well as healthy relationships. As I face the last years of life, I know that I will have pain from the previous bumps and added pain from future bumps. I have often had the feeling of the apostle Paul when he wrote, "For indeed, in this tent we groan, longing to be clothed with our dwelling from heaven. … For indeed, we who are in this tent groan, being burdened, because we do not want to be unclothed but to be clothed, so that what is mortal will be swallowed up by life" (2 Corinthians 5:2, 4). I share with Paul and many others the frustration, the decay, and the threat of death. My frailty makes me groan. While we are in our earthly existence, we long to have a perfect body. "How can I have hope for a perfect body?" "Will this better body come on earth?" Of course, the answer to the last question is "no." God has a future for his followers, which will include a new heaven and a new earth as well as a new body.

People long for immortality, survival, and reincarnation, and some even settle for annihilation, which means a nonexistence beyond death. Christianity has hope for suffering and death. It answers these issues with Christ's resurrection from the dead, which introduced the bodily resurrection of those who follow him. Resurrection is consistently seen in the New Testament as a demonstration of God's power over death. God raised Jesus from the dead, and because of Jesus' victory over death, believers will be raised from the dead. Yes, there is hope for help in my earthly existence, and there is hope for a resurrection body after I die.

The resurrection of Jesus is central in the teaching of Scripture. The apostle Paul gave a helpful discussion about Christ's resurrection and the Christian's resurrection in 1 Corinthians 15:1–58. Paul begins to write about the resurrection in 15:1–11. He starts by reminding the readers of the content of the gospel that he had preached to them (15:1–4).

First, Christ died for our sins. His death is at the heart of the gospel. Second, he was buried. This confirmed the reality of the death and resurrection of Jesus. The burial of Jesus' body was a prelude to the empty tomb. Third, after dying and being buried, Christ rose from the dead. The reality expressed with the phrase "rose again" has been translated by Leon Morris as "he has been raised."[5] The passive voice points to the activity of the Father in raising the Son. The perfect tense points to Jesus' continuing state. It sets forth with the utmost possible emphasis the abiding results of the event. Christ continues in the character of the risen Lord.[6]

Paul then spells out the historical basis for his witness to the risen Lord (1 Corinthians 15:4–7a). He mentions the appearance of Christ to Cephas, to the twelve, to more than five hundred people, to James, to all the apostles, and finally to Paul himself. The Christian faith is not based on wishful thinking but on the fact that God raised Jesus from the dead. Paul comments further on his experience with Christ on Damascus Road. "He appeared to me also," he says (1 Corinthians 15:7b–11). He thinks of himself as the last of those who saw the Lord, referring to himself as "untimely born." He may be referring to his unnatural entrance into the band of the apostles. From Paul's personal experience with Christ, he learned two things: respect for the office of an apostle and his profound sense of unworthiness to be an apostle. More than likely, this unworthiness existed in him because he persecuted the followers of Christ. He ascribed his acceptance and his service for God to the grace of God.

Paul reminds the Corinthians in verses 1 through 11 that they have been saved by a gospel to which the resurrection of Christ is central. Then, he tells readers that Jesus' resurrection was the basis of Christian hope (1 Corinthians 15:12–19). Apparently, the Corinthians had not questioned the resurrection of Christ, but they did question the future resurrection of believers. Notice Paul's emphatic point: "But if there is no resurrection of the dead, then not even Christ has been raised" (15:13). The resurrection of Christ and the resurrection of Christians stand or fall together; to deny one is to deny the other.

To deny the resurrection is to strip the Christian message of seven essentials. First, "if the dead are not raised, then not even Christ has been raised" (15:16). If there is no such thing as a resurrection, then Jesus did not triumph over death. Second, "if Christ has not been raised, then our preaching is vain" (15:14). The Christian gospel is based on the resurrection of Jesus Christ from the dead. If he was not raised, Christian preaching is false. Third, "if Christ has not been raised, your faith is worthless" (15:17). The collapse of the Christians' preaching would mean the collapse of their faith. Fourth, "we are even found to be false witnesses of God, because we have testified against God that He raised Christ" (15:15a). The reputation and character of God is destroyed if there is no resurrection. Fifth, "if Christ has not been raised…you are still in your sins" (15:17). The sin problem would remain unsolved. Sixth, if Christ has not been raised, "those who have fallen asleep in Christ have perished" (15:18). An awful consequence of there being no resurrection is that death would be forever. Seventh, "if we have hoped in Christ only in this life, we are of all people most to be pitied" (15:19). If life here on this earth is all there is, it makes no sense to base our hope on God. If the Christian faith is based on an empty gospel, anybody is better off than the Christian.[7]

We can now breathe a sigh of relief from the suppositions about no resurrection of Christ or of Christians. We hear a cry of confidence from Paul in 1 Corinthians 15:20–28. Paul paints an optimistic picture of God's ultimate supremacy. He answers our question, "Is there any hope after death?" Paul emphatically says yes with confidence: "But the fact is, Christ has been raised from the dead, the first fruits of those who are asleep" (15:20). A new age has dawned with the resurrection of Christ from the dead. He is the "first fruits" of a coming immense harvest of all those who have died "in Christ." The phrase "first fruits" means that Jesus was the first to rise from the dead, and it is clear that those who have died "in Christ" will also be raised from the dead.

In verses 21–22, Paul introduces the theme of the first and the last Adam. The first Adam introduced death to the human race because of his sin, and the result is that all people live in a self-centered and sinful world, with death as their lot. The last Adam, Christ, does not lead people to death but offers life through his resurrection. Through faith, every person may be in Christ and thus be members of his body. They are given a new existence. At his second coming, those who belong to Christ will be given the resurrection existence. This will include all Christians who are alive at his coming and all Christians who have died previously. Christ's second coming marks the final destruction of everything aimed against God—every rule, authority, and power. Only then will death—the last enemy—finally be robbed of its power.

If the major consequences of Christ's resurrection bear on the future and on eternity, then they must also bear on the present. First, Paul mentioned the practice of baptism with the resurrection of Jesus (15:29–34). If there is no resurrection of Christ, there is no reason to practice baptism (15:29). Second, Paul persevered in ministry despite the dangers he faced because of Christ's resurrection power in him (15:30–32a). He endured hardships because he was convinced that something infinitely better awaited him in the future—the resurrection power of Jesus sustained him through the most daunting experiences. The third and final consequence of the resurrection mention by Paul is pragmatic. If Christians surrender faith in the resurrection, they are opening the door to lax moral behavior. Wrong thinking, about the resurrection or any other fundamental articles of faith, inevitably leads to wrong behavior.

The glorious future to which Paul refers in 1 Corinthians 15:1–34 virtually defies all human understanding and description. In verses 35 through 50, Paul reaches the ultimate view of hope, a future resurrected body. The fact of a body's decomposition, humanly thinking, seems to rule out any possibility of a resurrection of the body. Paul answers questions about this future human resurrection: "But someone will say, 'How are the dead raised? And with what kind of body do they come?'" (1 Corinthians 15:35). Paul answers these questions in the following verses, and through all the answers runs one fundamental principle: "flesh and blood cannot inherit the kingdom of God" (15:50). Our physical bodies are incapable of coping with the glory of God. If we are to be resurrected in Christ, we need to be transformed into his likeness. Only Christlike people will be suitable for such a quality of life. Yet, however radical such a transformation, there will be a clear continuity between Christians now and Christians then. We shall be raised, not destroyed and transformed in a different existence.

Paul uses the metaphor of a seed and a plant (15:36–38). He shows that the Creator God is accustomed to producing many varied kinds of bodies, each perfectly suited to its own location. Paul illustrates how a seed is buried and how, afterwards, something different—a plant—comes from it. In the same way, our physical bodies, ideal for this earthly existence in spite of their mortality, will be useless in the perfection of God's kingdom. They need to die and be buried so that God can produce a spiritual body perfectly suited for life in God's kingdom.

In verses 42 through 44, Paul gives four antitheses to show the difference between the body that dies and the body that is raised from the dead. First, the body that dies is perishable, or subject to decay, because it is part of a world that is subject to corruption. In contrast, the body that is raised is imperishable, free from corruption, and able to realize the fullness of the life willed by the Creator. Second, the body that is buried is characterized by dishonor or humiliation and wretchedness. The body that is raised is marked by glory or splendor in accordance with the character of God. Third, the body that dies is characterized by weakness, physical and spiritual, and is the victim of death, while the body that is raised is marked by power or strength. This power is given by the One who has the power to raise the dead. Fourth, the body that dies is a physical body, subject to frailty and mortality. The body that is raised is animated by the Spirit of God.

In 1 Corinthians 15:45–49, Paul contrasts the physical bodies of humans, who are descendants of Adam, with the spiritual bodies that will be given to those being transformed in the image of Christ. A spiritual body is one that is made vital by the Spirit and fit to be in the presence of God in the age to come. A physical body is appropriate in this present age, but a spiritual body will be appropriate in the age to come.

Paul concludes his discussion of the new world and the new body with a brief summary and an exciting celebration in 1 Corinthians 15:50–58. He contrasts the body that expresses itself in earthly life with the body that will eventually express the supernatural life of God's Spirit in God's kingdom. It is obvious that the earthly body (flesh and blood) cannot inherit the kingdom of God because decay and corruption cannot be part of what is eternally incorruptible. Paul struggles to describe the indescribable. Who can imagine a body without weakness? Or disease? Or tiredness? Or death?[8] The Christian dead will be raised imperishable, no longer subject to corruption. Life in the age to come requires an imperishable nature and an immortality. When we think about it, this future existence is unimaginable—but it is gloriously true.

The section on the resurrection comes to a magnificent climax. The promise of this new body calls for thanksgiving to God, the source of the victory. Paul speaks about telling "a mystery" in verse 51. This is a word used to describe an open secret revealed by the Spirit. What was unveiled to Paul came by special revelation. It is what will happen at Christ's final return to earth. Paul uses the word "sleep" to describe believers who die before the return of Christ. Many believers will be alive at the coming of Christ. Both groups, those who are dead and those who are alive, will be changed from having earthly bodies to having spiritual bodies. The Lord's return makes a transition for God's people from time into eternity. It marks the consummation of things temporal and inaugurates things eternal. This change comes with a suddenness—in a moment, in the twinkling of an eye, at the last trumpet. It marks the end of all things as we know them.[9]

Paul leads a celebration that the power of death is undone and the sting of sin has been taken away. Human beings are in the bondage of the law, sin, and death. But Christ sets believers free from all of these bondages. Because death has been robbed of its terror, a Christian can live with confidence, courage, and commitment. These truths cause Christians to give thanks and to celebrate.

Eugene O'Neill dramatizes the truth of the defeat of death in his play, *Lazarus Laughed*. He tells how the brother of Mary and Martha, who was raised from the dead, leaves his old home in Bethany and journeys to Greece. In a square in Athens, he meets the half-crazed and utterly cruel Gaius Caligula, who has been chosen by the Emperor Tiberius as his successor. When spies inform Caligula that the people hate him, he retorts, "Let them hate—so long as they fear us! We must keep death dangling before their eyes…I like to watch men die." Suddenly this wicked monster of a man is confronted by Lazarus, who has the appearance of a stranger from a far land. Caligula accuses Lazarus of teaching people to laugh at death and threatens him with execution. But Lazarus looks into Caligula's face and laughs softly, "Death is dead, Caligula, Death is dead."[10]

How do I close a chapter on Christian hope? How do I give a final word about pain and suffering in this book? Paul provides a good closing in Romans 8:18: "For I consider that the sufferings of this present time are not worthy to be compared with the glory that is to be revealed to us." The believer's earthly existence will be in a body subject to disease and decay, but the believer's future will be given a new body and a perfect world in which to live. The magnificence of God's future glory will greatly surpass the unpleasantness of our suffering in the present world. Pain today—perfection tomorrow. That is the greatest hope I know.

## Notes

[1] Written by Russell Kelso Carter, tune PROMISES, 1886, public domain.

[2] John R. W. Stott, *Romans: God's Good News for the World* (Downers Grove, IL: InterVarsity Press, 1994), 238.

[3] A. M. Hunter, *The Epistle to the Romans: Introduction and Commentary*. London: SCM Press LTD, 1955), p. 83.

[4] Bruce M. Metzger, *Breaking the Code: Understanding the Book of Revelation* (Nashville: Abingdon Press, 1993), 100.

[5] Leon Morris, "The First Epistle of Paul to the Corinthians: An Introduction and Commentary," in *Tyndale Bible Commentaries* (Grand Rapids: Wm. B. Eerdmans Publishing Company, 1970), 205.

[6] Ibid., 206.

[7] Ibid., 212.

[8] David Prior, "The Message of I Corinthians," in *The Bible Speaks Today* (Downers Grove, IL: 1985), 274.

[9] Ibid., 275–76.

[10] Eugene O'Neill, *Lazarus Laughed* (New York: Random House, 1925).

www.ingramcontent.com/pod-product-compliance
Lightning Source LLC
Chambersburg PA
CBHW071007160426
43193CB00012B/1954